THE POSITIVITY CODE

SUPERCHARGE YOUR LIFE WITH POSITIVE THINKING

*Learn The Art of Positive Thinking, Changing
Your Life One Thought at a Time*

Chrío Zoë

ZOË PUBLISHING

Acknowledgement

Writing this book has been a labor and a journey that I couldn't have undertaken without the incredible support and encouragement of many individuals. I am profoundly grateful to all those who have played a part in bringing this project to fruition.

I would like to thank each person who was instrumental in shaping my path to writing this manuscript. My sincerest appreciation goes to the countless friends and family who graciously gave me space and time to make this book become a reality.

First and foremost, I want to express my deepest gratitude to my family whose unwavering belief in me and constant encouragement have been my driving force. Your love and support have sustained me through the challenges of this creative process. I give honor to my late parents, Stephen and Pearl, whose unwavering belief has been the catalyst to propel me in this journey. Their constant encouragement and unconditional love have been my strength to pursue this endeavor. I say thank you to my siblings Michael, Anthony, Pauline and Sharon who have now passed on but are the silent voices that ignited me to write this book. Through their life, in their own small contributing way, I have come to realize that this journey we call life is valuable and how we start the journey does not dictate how we finish it.

I would like to thank all of my mentors and teachers who helped me by sharing their invaluable knowledge base with me, as they guided me from a place of knowing in shaping my ideas and refining my writing. I cherish your warm guidance, encouragement, and belief in me, and my potential and I can attest to the fact that it has been transformative. I am sincerely hoping that this book will serve as a helpful resource and companion guide on my readers' journey toward self-improvement, empowerment, and fulfillment.

I'd also like to thank the team at AIA and Publishing Services for their dedication and hard work in bringing this book to life. Your expertise coaching and guidance in outlining, design, formatting, and marketing have been pivotal in turning my manuscript into a polished publication.

Additionally, I am grateful to my dear friends, who provided much-needed moral support and encouragement during the writing process. I am forever grateful for your influence and for your push to encourage me into what you believe I could be. Thank you all for the guidance and the wisdom you shared with me as I stumbled along my sometimes-rocky road of personal growth and self-discovery. I extend my heartfelt appreciation to my friends and colleagues who provided valuable feedback, engaged in insightful discussions, and cheered me on during moments of doubt. Your enthusiasm has been contagious and uplifting.

Finally, I want to acknowledge my readers—those who will engage with this book. Your curiosity and interest in my ideas fuel my passion for writing, and I hope this book resonates with you in meaningful ways. In writing this book, I've come to realize that the journey is made sweeter by the presence of supportive souls. To all those I've mentioned and to anyone whose name might have been inadvertently omitted, please know that your impact has been immeasurable.

To all of you, your enthusiasm, engagement, and support to me have been more than appreciated. Let me end by saying once again to my readers that I applaud you for buying this book to enhance and empower your personal development. I trust that this book will meet your desire.

With heartfelt thanks,

Chrío Zoë

Contents

Introduction

Most of you are probably familiar with the idea that our mind plays a huge part in controlling our bodies. But what exactly does that mean? Maintaining control of your mind will play a huge role in your psychological and physiological well-being. When you embrace positivity, it enables you to handle your day-to-day activities better and will also help you to handle situations you cannot control or unexpected events that can significantly change your mood or the function of your life. I am in no way saying to live in a delusional or unrealistic bubble; what this concept means is that it will open you to optimism, minimize worry and anxiety, and drown out negative thoughts. Together, let's embark on this journey to explore the true potential of positive thinking and uncover the secrets to crafting a joyful and satisfying life flowing with abundance. I know the impact positive thinking has, as I have embraced it, and it has changed my mindset and how I operate. This is why I felt the need to share this with others. I firmly believe that by managing our thoughts effectively, we can transform the narrative we construct in our minds and manifest our aspirations.

The world today has many challenging and unfortunate incidents unfolding before our eyes. I understand and acknowledge both the existence and importance of how various incidents impact your life. My aim is not to make your challenges seem less important. Instead, I want to provide you with the tools you need and help shift your mindset in a way that helps you deal with and overcome these challenges with a strong belief that things will turn out well. When we encounter obstacles, it will consume our minds to the point that we lose focus on other things, and then we drift into the ocean of hopelessness, and before we know it, we are struggling to perform our daily tasks. I strongly believe that by tapping into the power of positivity, you can overcome these difficulties without throwing in the towel, losing hope, and losing yourself. In this book, I will outline techniques that will empower you, and through this newfound empowerment, you will conquer adversity while safeguarding your happiness and overall well-being. You will discover a new level of growth and self-improvement that will assist you in living a life that brings joy and fulfillment. I will be providing you with a set of principles that, when you start practicing them, will steer you toward changing your mindset and will improve your life in a profound manner. You will have to open your mind and embrace it, as it is the key to unlocking the door of possibilities and enlightenment. The knowledge you will gain from reading this book will feed your garden of wisdom, and the soil will be filled with empowerment that will make all the fruits and flowers of your garden grow. You will learn to take charge of your thoughts and emotions after reading this book, as it is not filled with fairytale promises and fleeting motivation.

Each chapter has been thoughtfully crafted to help you on this journey. I will provide you with not just insight but practical exercises and real-life examples that will inspire you to adopt a growth mindset. Prepare yourself for an adventure of self-discovery and the opportunity to transform your life. My aim is for you to rewire your mind with positivity and resilience by dispelling any limiting beliefs that have hindered your progress. Your mind will instead be filled with empowering beliefs that will propel you forward. Always remember to be kind to yourself along the way. Keep in mind that this will not happen overnight; it will take time and effort. The main thing is that you remain consistent; you are making a change to how you have been thinking for years. So please be patient with yourself. I encourage you to remain mindful, embrace your journey, and have confidence in the process. The road to self-discovery will have hiccups, but it is undoubtedly worthwhile. The Positivity Code possesses the power to unlock a life brimming with abundance, happiness, and fulfillment.

Chapter 1

Discovering Yourself

Self-discovery plays a huge role in your path to acquiring a positive mindset. And fully understanding who you truly are. The truth is that the majority of us want to live a life that is filled with purpose and meaning. Being helpful to those around you is a core part of living a purposeful and meaningful life. When you feel as if you have no purpose or value, that is also what will feed that tree of negativity. So, in order to find peace and happiness and start channeling positivity, you need to understand yourself better. To accomplish this, you will need to overcome somewhat of a lingering contradiction that some of you may be dealing with, which is that you may be familiar with things about you that make you, YOU. And contribute to your personality. However, you may not truly understand yourself or who you are. Seriously, how much do you really know about yourself? Now, some of you may be reading this and ready to tell me what kind of personality traits you possess. However, I am not referring to the results of your personality test that you took last week or last year or going on ancestry.com to learn about your family history (I mean, nothing is wrong with this). We should all look into our family lineage to gain knowledge, but this is not what makes you, YOU. I am also not referring to what colors you love that spark excitement in your soul when you are choosing curtains for your space, or who your best friend is, or what your life was like in high school or college. Now that I have gone through the top things that people feel contribute to knowing themselves, I can get down to where I am leading you all too. What I am referring to is something bigger and more important.

Please note that I am not saying that the things listed (family, friends, personality, experiences, etc.) are not important; however, sometimes, because we are unaware of who we truly are, we tend to treat or deal with the things listed in a negative way and are not even sure why. So I am referring to your true self, the things that make your soul come alive, the activities that feed your soul and make you feel excited and energized, the things that bring you happiness, and the things that make you feel tired or demotivated. I will explain how to distinguish between these things so you can make good choices as you progress in life. The thing is, there are many people who do not know who they truly are, but their lives are in alignment, and it is really because of chance or luck. And that, my dear readers, is too dangerous of a risk for you to take, so I would rather remove that from your mind frame altogether. I do not want any of you to have lives that align with chance or luck but deliberately, intentionally, and purposefully. How can you achieve this? You can achieve this by becoming familiar with who you truly are. You can start by figuring out what is important to you, what you enjoy doing, and what you want to achieve. Another way is to make sure you are asking yourself the correct questions.

Self-Discovery Questions

Here are some questions that can help you start a meaningful conversation with yourself. I want you all to answer these questions truthfully; do not try to figure out what sounds good or looks good on paper. You will not be graded, and I won't be seeing these responses. When you are ready to start, make sure you are in a quiet space without any distractions. Take a few deep breaths to relax yourself, clear your mind of any thoughts or disturbances, and begin. Also, I want you to keep in mind that there are no correct or incorrect answers.

This is just you discovering how to become closer to yourself.

1. What activity in your life makes you really happy?

2. What is something you always enjoy doing, even when you are tired or in a hurry? Why do you like it?

3. If you are not happy in a relationship or job, do you decide to stay or go? If you decide to stay, why is that?

4. What makes you afraid of quitting a terrible job or ending a toxic relationship?

5. What do you think you can achieve?

6. What is one thing you have done in your life that truly makes you feel the most proud?

7. What is the second thing that you have done in your life that you are most proud of?

8. What kind of impact or reputation do you want to leave behind after you are gone?

9. How does your presence in the universe make humanity better?

10. If you could make one wish come true, what would you wish for?

11. How comfortable are you with the fact that one day you will die?

12. What is the most important thing to you in life right now?

13. How do you think other people view you?

14. How do you want people to view you?

15. How sure are you of yourself that you can make your own decisions?

16. What is the biggest belief about yourself that holds you back?

17. Who is the most significant person in your life?

18. Who do you admire and look up to the most?

19. The person you admire and look up to the most—do you wish that you were like them? Or do you want to be like them?

20. If you answered yes above, why do you wish you were like them? Or why do you want to be like them?

21. Who is someone you spend time with even though you don't like them?

22. Why do you spend time with them even though you do not fancy their company?

23. What is something that is always true for you, regardless of the circumstances you may be facing?

24. What guides you in making hard choices based on what is right or wrong?

25. What is a mistake that you have made that ended up teaching you something valuable?

26. Have you repeat that mistake again?

27. How does gratitude impact your life?

28. What are your thoughts and emotions towards your parents?

29. Are you good at handling money?

30. Do you save money well?

31. Do you overspend even though you may be in a tight financial situation?

32. If you answered yes, why do you believe you do that?

33. Do you pay your bills on time?

34. If you find that you do not pay your bills on time, why is that?

35. If you were to choose between paying your rent on time and buying a new device, which would you choose?

36. How do you feel about aging?

37. How has getting an education affected your life, and what do you think about it?

38. Do you think your future is already decided, or can you decide your own fate?

39. What do you think is the purpose or reason for your existence?

Yes, I am aware; this is a lot to digest and think about. I am not trying to sound harsh or mean, but these questions were not intended to be simple or comfortable. It is crucial for you to ask yourself these questions to gain a deeper understanding of yourself.

The process of self-discovery starts by asking yourself these questions. If you have never done it before, it can be uncomfortable and even strange in the beginning, but it gets easier with time. Even enjoyable. Yes, I said enjoyable because you will be getting to know yourself. You may not be aware of this, but I want all of you to know that you are wise, astute, and brilliant. You are intriguing and profound. You have talent, and you are gifted. You have limitless ability to achieve your goals. You are not ugly, nor are you too old. You are not overly dull or slow.

Simply put, none of the awful things you tell yourself about yourself exist. You are the complete opposite. You are ample and sufficient. You can, therefore, judge whether or not this journey of self-discovery is valuable, but I assure you that it is. Knowing yourself is a worthy endeavor. Get those pens or pencils out, and just do it! You can do it, and I believe in you! Also, you do not have to answer all the questions at once; take your time. So, get into the positivity car and prepare for the most thrilling trip of your life!

Chapter 2

The Power of Positive Thinking

Your mind can help you achieve many things. From thinking that you are capable of doing a difficult task to learning a new language, you will find that you will, in fact, be successful in tackling this new challenge, and if you do not do well the first time, you will develop such resilience that you will go at it again, as you have conditioned your mind into thinking that you can do it. This is why positive thinking is something you should embrace. Positive thinking is not about ignoring your emotions when you are sad or facing a major challenge. What positive thinking does is place you in a state where you approach these issues in a more productive and constructive way. Being hopeful is one key point to this mindset, as is learning to accept certain things and situations that you have no control over. There are many times that you may end up feeling worse or hopeless because you are trying to change something that simply cannot be changed. What this does is place your mind in a state of restlessness. You will gain no peace by doing this.

The power of positive thinking lies in maintaining an empowering outlook on life. When you decide to shift your mindset to that of a way of thinking, you will find that you will approach various situations with resilience and optimism and gain a problem-solving attitude. With time and practice, making this mindset a part of you will allow you to embrace the best that life has to offer and lean towards expecting positive outcomes. You will be less focused on always preparing for worst-case scenarios and floating in the sea of negativity. You will start to picture yourself obtaining success, being truly happy, and having good health. Success and happiness will no longer seem as if they are unattainable, and you will develop your own standards as it pertains to happiness and success, as having a positive mindset helps you to truly appreciate and understand yourself on a deep level as opposed to comparing yourself to others and feeling as if you are a failure. You will choose to embrace new growth, and you will venture into trying new things without being fearful. This newfound optimism will empower you as you face challenges and new life experiences. You may be reading this and love how it sounds, but you are still wondering where to start. Well, positive thinking starts with self-talk. We all have an inner voice that streams a series of thoughts in our minds that we do not say out loud. These thoughts that come to your mind automatically tend to be positive and negative; however, there is always one that is more dominant. There are some things that you tell yourself that make a lot of sense and are grounded in logic. There are times that the things you say to yourself are not factual because you do not have the actual facts or because you have a certain version of what happened. For instance, someone with body dysmorphia will see and think that they are fat or overweight when that is not the actual case, but they constantly tell themselves this. If you water the negativity plant more than the positive vibes plant, it will grow and gain dominance in your mind, and you will only have a negative outlook on life. Your positive vibes plant will be dry, and the leaves will fall off and eventually die, which is what I do not want for any of you.

If you water and nourish your positive vibes plant, you will become an optimist and believe in positive thinking. The goal I want for you all is to stop feeding the negativity plant. It needs to become dry for the leaves to fall off. By practicing positive thinking, you can transform your mindset by seeking out and amplifying the better aspects of your life. You will start seeing setbacks in your life as they detour along your path of growth, success, and happiness. I am sure that none of you want to remain in a vortex of hopelessness and feel trapped by negative thoughts. Relying on factors and circumstances to shape your happiness will limit you, and it will keep you a prisoner in your own mind, which will limit your growth and true potential. Here's why relying on circumstances or factors to be the key to your happiness is setting yourself up to fall into a whirlpool of hopelessness because if the circumstances do not work out, what will that mean for you? You will end up feeling as if you failed, and when you probably did not, you will start feeling as if you cannot achieve happiness because of that circumstance or factor. Having a positive mindset will not allow you to feel trapped by circumstances or factors. What it does is free you from placing so much power into things that determine whether you are happy or not, whether you are at peace or not. Having this mindset makes you happy, regardless of the outcome. Practicing this mindset will free your mind and release you from falling into hopelessness because something did not work out or because you failed at something. Your positivity garden will flourish as you gain more insight into yourself by accepting situations when they do not work and finding true inner peace. You will find that your thoughts are more constructive and solution-based.

Implementing a positive mindset significantly impacts your physiological and psychological well-being. Having a positive mindset boosts your self-esteem and strengthens your relationships with work colleagues, friends, family members, your children, your health, and your partner. When you interact with people in general, people will find you more approachable.

Positive thinking can affect your health in good ways, such as:

- ☞ You will increase your life span as you will not develop certain stress-related issues.

- ☞ It lowers your chance of developing depression.

- ☞ It lowers your distress rate.

- ☞ Your resilience to illness increases.

- ☞ Improved psychological and physiological health.

- ☞ Improved heart health and reduced the risk of dying from heart disease and stroke.

- ☞ Having good coping skills means being able to handle difficult situations and times when you feel overwhelmed or upset.

- ☞ You will notice a rise in your creativity.

Please do not place any pressure on yourself, as this will not happen overnight; it will take time and consistency, and I cannot stress this enough.

Examine the Negative Thoughts in Your Mind

Before you embark on your positive mindset journey, you are going to need to examine the negative thoughts in your mind. If not, you will find that your journey will be a bit more challenging. Some of these negative thoughts include:

- ☞ **Magnifying**: You may find that you tend to make a huge deal out of minor situations.

- ☞ **Perfectionism**: There are many people who struggle with this, and this can leave you stuck if not addressed, as you set unrealistic and impossible standards, and trying to be perfect often sets you up for failure.

- ☞ **Polarizing**: This is also known as seeing things either black or white; there is no gray area for you. This makes you less open to compromise or finding alternate ways to approach things.

- ☞ **Blaming yourself for everything**: Do you notice that you take the blame for something when something bad or disappointing occurs? For instance, if your partner declines a night out, you immediately assume that they do not want to spend time with you.

- ☞ **Expecting the worst**: You encounter a minor setback, and you immediately start preparing yourself for the worse. You do an examination at the doctor's office, and you start thinking the results are going to be bad. If one morning your car does not start, you believe that your entire day is going to be bad.

As I have stated, this way of thinking will not disappear overnight; however, once you begin to practice, you will get better at it.

How to Practice Positive Thinking

The moment you feel that you have gotten a handle on making the loud voice of negativity silent, try these methods as you embark on your positivity journey:

- **Check on yourself**: I know you probably paused and made sure that you read that correctly. What I mean by this is, at some point during the day, evaluate your thought process. If you notice that they are mostly negative, take some time and implant some positivity in your mind.

- **Be open to humor**: Allow yourself to smile or laugh, even during difficult times. If there is a catchphrase that always makes you laugh, try to make it a part of your everyday life. When you embrace humor, you find that you are less stressed out.

- **Reframe your situation**: When something happens that you cannot control, I know it is your nature to want it fixed immediately. But take that time to appreciate the upside. For instance, if it is raining and you are stuck in traffic, you are getting irritated because you want to get home. When you notice this, pause and appreciate that you are not outside in the rain walking to get to the bus stop. Also, appreciate that you have a car. Play some songs that you love, or turn on a podcast.

☞ **Follow a healthy lifestyle**: This is influential on your journey towards positivity. Your goal should be to exercise for about 30 minutes at least three times a week. Not only does exercise play a role in minimizing stress, but it also helps you rest better at night. Eating healthy should be a factor for you, as should learning different techniques to manage stress.

☞ **Keep a gratitude journal**: This may seem tacky to some of you; however, writing down the things that you are truly grateful for will shift your focus, and you will see that there are many things in your life for you to be thankful for.

☞ **Surround yourself with positive people**: You do not need to do everything yourself; having positive people in your life will do wonders for you as they can encourage you and give positive and constructive feedback. Evaluate the people in your life and see if they have a negative mindset. Negative people have a way of increasing your stress level and clouding your mind when you are trying to make rational decisions and handle stress.

☞ **Practice positive self-talk**: The best way to do this is by not saying things to yourself that you would not say to a friend, family member, etc. I always emphasize being gentle with yourself, and I truly mean this, and you should really put this into practice. Be encouraging to yourself. If negative thoughts creep into your mind, find ways to rationally evaluate them and counter them with positive affirmations and things you are thankful for.

☞ **Focus on your strengths**: Each day, think about something that you consider to be your personal strength. You may not have ever thought about this before, but your personal strengths can be kindness, being creative, being structured, being a team player, completing things you start, etc. Whatever your personal strength is, plan ways to use it in a new way, then act on it. It will do wonders for your mood and attitude. With practice, you can add more positive thoughts to your life and enjoy the benefits that come with optimism.

Misconceptions About Positive Thinking

There are many misconceptions that may cloud your understanding of positive thinking. In this section, I will debunk some of these common misconceptions to give you better clarification and understanding.

☞ **Positive thinking means ignoring the negative**: This is not true. Thinking that having a positive mindset means that you block out all negativity is not realistic. If you ignore your issues, push them aside, and place a fake smile on your face, it will not help you. What I want you all to know is that nothing is wrong with feeling overwhelmed and that negative feelings are all part of being a human being. The key point is how you respond to these feelings, instead of placing them on a wheelbarrow and rolling them down a hill and running in the opposite direction and not being your true self. The aim of having this new mentality is that, instead of ignoring them, it focuses more on how you handle them, allowing yourself to tap into understanding why they are present and then understanding how to deal with them. So it is not about denying them but gaining knowledge of how to steer through them, and not having them makes you feel stuck and hopeless.

☞ **Having a positive mindset leads to success**: Thinking positively will not make success drop in your lap. What I want to make clear is that success takes time and work. What positivity does is help feed your drive and not make you feel that you cannot achieve your goal. So, rather than imagining success and working out worst-case scenarios, you are more inclined to take action and stay with the plan you laid out to achieve your end goal.

☞ **Positive thinking is hard to learn**: This is not factual. Don't get me wrong, there are people who have a natural positive outlook on life. However, just because you need to deprogram and learn this new mindset, it is difficult. It may be challenging. But that is okay; challenges are a part of life. You will now be taking on self-awareness, challenging your old way of thinking, and making a conscious effort to shift your perspectives. With practice and commitment, you can adopt this mindset as well. Do not write it off because you feel it will be difficult to learn.

☞ **Positive affirmations instantly work**: Positive affirmations are very helpful; do not get me wrong. However, if you start your journey thinking that they will instantly work, you are going to frustrate yourself. If you select affirmations that are not close to your current situation, you will find that they are not connecting with you. So, what do you do? Choose affirmations that are more relevant to your situation. Because if you don't, instead of motivating you, it will seem far-fetched, and you will be disappointed. Choose affirmations that feel real to you and are geared toward truly inspiring you and helping you reach your goals instead of just waiting for them to magically come to you.

☞ **Having a positive mindset means you will no longer need professional counseling**: There are some of you who may be struggling mentally and emotionally. Whereas positive thinking is a very powerful tool, it is not wise to abandon medication if you are taking it for your mental illness or any other professional help. Positive thinking will shift your outlook, but it is in no way a cure for mental illness. Do not abandon any professional help you are receiving. They can work together. You will have a better grip on life if you allow them to work in sync.

☞ **Positive thinking and naivety are twins**: There is a common misconception that having a positive mindset is the same as being naïve and that you are living in a bubble. This is far from the truth. Having a positive mindset is not about ignoring what is happening around you and being naive. It is actually the total opposite. I have highlighted many things about having this mindset, and there is a common word I use a lot, and that is resilience. Positive thinking allows you to see possible solutions in very difficult and trying situations.

☞ **Positive thinking means that you should always be doing positive activities 24/7**: You may feel that once you adopt this new mindset. You should be the positivity superhero, thinking you should be practicing yoga mixed with reading five self-help books per month plus working on your goals mixed with volunteer work and spreading positive messages all day. If you take on that all at once, you will burn out. Here is the thing: You do not have to be super productive all the time. Finding time to rest, relax, and make time for yourself is just as important. Allow yourself to slow down.

Chapter 3

Believing in Yourself

Believing in yourself is a key component of your positive thinking journey. There are times when your self-doubt can hinder you from reaching your true potential. I would like for you to unlock the door to believing in yourself. Believing in yourself encompasses trusting what you can do. When you have true faith in yourself, you can tackle uncertainty and self-doubt head-on and have the courage to face challenging tasks. This is why it has to be something you unlock as you adopt this new mindset. I have listed ways in which you can work towards believing in yourself right now.

Focus on Your Strengths

When you fail repeatedly at something that appears easy for others, it gets kind of hard to believe in yourself. When you start to lose confidence in yourself, you will find that you dwell on your limitations. It is because, during this time, your sense of weakness is more acute. Please do not think you are the only one who goes through this because you are not. This feeling sucks! Failure, weakness, and shame are severely emphasized in your memory. If you allow yourself to marinate on it, this is where the negative tree gets strength because you are watering it with thoughts like "I'm not good at this," which then manifests into "I'll never be good at anything!" Everyone has strengths and shortcomings, so you are not designed differently. To make the most of your strengths, you must learn how to recognize them. That word, recognizing, is going to become your new best friend. The way forward is not only adopting a positive mindset but also building your confidence level.

You can feed the confidence plant in your garden of wisdom by:

A. Putting an end to wasting time on stuff you are not wired for.

B. Determine your areas of strength and focus on honing them.

Let me share something with you: Many successful people frequently assign their shortcomings to others instead of frustrating themselves with tasks that they cannot do or are not necessarily good at. No, they are not being quitters; they are being efficient and smart, so if there is someone on the team who excels at programming and they may not be that great at it, they will pass that task to the team member who can do programming in their sleep and concentrate on their strengths rather than thinking about their shortcomings. This helps them avoid feeling inadequate or as if they cannot get something right. Taking this approach, you will feel instantly more capable and confident when you turn your attention to playing to your strengths. Furthermore, you can truly succeed if you work to enhance your innate skills. Some of your strengths may already be known to you; there are others you may not have tapped into.

Consider the following to help you come up with some ideas for how people may view you:

- ☞ Always has a broad-picture perspective and an optimistic outlook

- ☞ Observes the small details and is meticulous

- ☞ Enjoys education and investigation

- ☞ Skillful orator

- ☞ Remains persistent.

- ☞ Practical and driven by action

If you can, I suggest having a conversation about your strengths with your loved ones, close friends, and coworkers. What are some of the issues they bring to you for resolution? This activity can build confidence, but keep in mind that you're not looking for praise. You can focus more of your efforts on the areas where you already possess great talent if you are aware of your strong abilities. Your growth can follow your innate path. You can find the resources to take on any task once you are operating from a position of confidence and self-belief. Acknowledging your inherent strengths and weaknesses allows you to quit beating yourself up, and allowing negativity to take over does not provide solutions. You can focus on your strengths and devise solutions for the remaining tasks. For example, starting a business requires a variety of abilities, but not all of them are necessary.

Become Your Own Coach

If you do not have confidence in yourself, you will not trust or listen to someone encouraging you from the sidelines. This is why believing in yourself is integral to this journey. Think about it for a second: What makes a coach great? Or, what makes managers great and easy to deal with? They tend to empower you and not just give you orders but provide you with the right tools to succeed. Great coaches and leaders lead by example. It is not a dictatorship. Setting goals and adopting an optimistic outlook are not sufficient to produce results. What I am trying to say is that, yes, those things are what you should do. However, none of those things will help you if you do not think you are capable of achieving them. So this comes back to my point about becoming your own coach. Think about becoming the kind of coach who gives you so much encouragement and provides you with the tools that help you execute your plays. The only thing is that it is not for a team but for yourself! Each step that you take will bring you closer to watering your garden of wisdom and feeding your positive flowers. You are going to have to practice to stop being judgmental of yourself. Also, if you do not consider yourself a leader, I am here to tell you that you do not need to possess leadership qualities to guide yourself through this. It has to start with you believing in yourself and manifesting the idea that you are more than capable of becoming your own coach.

Embrace Who You Are

Remember how I started by telling you that you should get to know who you are? Now, once you have discovered who you truly are, you are to embrace the person you are. Some of you may discover that you were trying to be someone you are not. Gaining a better level of self-confidence and a positive mindset requires that you embrace who you are and what is important to you. This is not achieved by being fake or attempting to win people. The truth is, from an early age, there is a great push to "be normal" or "fit in." This was something that many of us carried with us into adulthood because we learned it so early. If your goal is to have a routine existence, then that is fine; it is your life. However, I believe that those of you who are reading this book are not cut out for that kind of life. I believe that you are looking for more. Your belief in your value, competence, and potential as a human being will emerge when you start to live authentically and according to your identity and basic values.

Your core values lay the groundwork for creating an internal framework that will direct your future behaviors. It is best to embrace yourself in tiny steps:

- ☞ Put your priorities down on paper first.

- ☞ This should be repeated multiple times over weeks or even months. You'll get closer to discovering your basic values.

- ☞ This will enable you to look past the ideas that you have been taught to accept as true. You'll have a list of characteristics that best capture who you are after you're done.

- ☞ Examine your cognitive and behavioral tendencies.

Do you frequently compromise your morals to appease others? If your response is yes, take into consideration your motivations when you feel like you are trying to maintain harmony or be kind. What happens is that, in the end, you become less confident in yourself and begin to prioritize the approval of others. This can become problematic in several ways, but this is how you end up comparing yourself to others. You will lose yourself because you are creating a persona that is not yours; you will start feeding the tree of negativity and self-doubt, and the list goes on. What I want from you is to break free from other people's expectations. Because it will hinder you on your journey of positive thinking, I know it feels risky to be genuine, and you may be worried about what people will think of you. Keep in mind that life is about you in your experience, and life is about you in theirs. Do not forget that little gem I left there. You will gain the confidence you need to be your authentic self by taking on challenges that terrify you. Being vulnerable means acknowledging your fear and not running from it, which may seem counterintuitive, but it is the best way to gain strength. Allocate time for experiences that deviate from your regular schedule. It might be picking up a paintbrush and joining a painting class, enrolling in a fitness class, or leaping out of an airplane. Choose an activity that sounds exciting but also makes you feel a little afraid, then go for it. These are exercises that will teach you so much about yourself that you ought to do them often. Mix it up and try something new frequently.

Believe That You Can and You Will

The most effective weapon you possess is your belief. Simply altering your beliefs can make a huge difference in your life. I hope this is where your AHA moment kicked in, and you successfully linked why this ties in with shifting your mindset. Believing something transforms how you see the world and yourself; this is not wishful thinking. You perceive either overwhelming obstacles or possibilities. Which one will you choose? You have to let go of the notion that your current way of thinking cannot be changed. This kind of thinking is known as a fixed mindset, and it will hinder your progress and growth. What I want is for all of you to realize that you believe change is achievable. The motivation behind all of your efforts comes from a strong conviction that you and your life are capable of improving. At that point, you will become more eager to put in the necessary effort to bring about such improvements. Observing the fruits of your labor is the best way to increase your confidence. However, if you do not think it is worth it, you will not try.

Identifying If You Have an Inferiority Complex

I am sure many of you have heard of or are familiar with the term inferiority complex. Many times, it is used out of context to insult someone, or some of you feel that you have it but are not sure. What I plan on doing is going into detail about it, and if you are someone who has an inferiority complex, I will be delving into how you can deal with it. It can play a major role in how we think and act. Many people, at some point in their lives, experience moments of feeling insignificant or inferior. It is a normal thing that happens, as we are all human beings. When we look at people or rather admire people who are sports stars, celebrities, successful business moguls, famous scientists, coworkers who are doing really well, etc. This is normal for many of us; it gives us some level of motivation, or we just simply appreciate them for their contributions to society. In some cases, as it pertains to athletes, we may want to try some of the workout routines so that we can do better on a fitness level. However, it gets unhealthy when it has shifted from admiration to feeling inadequate to these people and that you have not achieved anything in your own life, and those feelings of not being good enough become too much or start making our lives worse. It might mean you have an inferiority complex. The American Psychology Association describes it as a fundamental sense of feeling inadequate or insecure that stems from real or perceived physical or psychological deficiencies. It can manifest behaviorally in a variety of ways, from the withdrawal of paralyzing fear to the excess compensation of exasperated rivalry and aggression. It is crucial to know that there are two ways a person responds when having an inferiority complex: Either they overcompensate by becoming very competitive in an attempt to prove they are not inferior. Or the person becomes so reclusive that they rarely engage with others. Occasionally, the second kind may also manifest as an excessive sense of superiority.

Inferiority Complex Symptoms

There are other symptoms that you may be displaying that are not signs of an inferiority complex. If you frequently find yourself feeling inferior to others and it is negatively impacting your life, you may be suffering from an inferiority complex. You can believe that you are not as good as the others in your peer group in terms of intelligence, looks, social skills, or psychological makeup. Being inferior can be a very lonely feeling. Look below and check if any of what I listed applies to you.

- ☞ **The tiniest critique leaves you feeling depressed for several days**: It could be that you went to the doctor and you were experiencing a stomach ache, and when the doctor examined you and told you that you were fine with just a slight indigestion, you needed to lose five pounds to be at a more balanced weight and that really had you feeling at your worst.

- ☞ **You are a stickler for detail, so nothing is ever quite right**: You could be hosting an event, and you notice that one of the napkins at one of the tables is not folded correctly. You will probably go and fold it and all the others at the table so that it is done the "correct" way.

- ☞ **You have the impression of being an outsider looking in, as though you are different**: You could be around your coworkers, and they are saying they like a particular series on Netflix; they are all saying pretty much the same thing about the show; however, you do not like the show and cannot identify with what is happening. Due to this, you feel like a total outsider.

- ☞ **You suffer from a pervasive sense of unworthiness and inadequacy**: Regardless of what you may have accomplished, you always have a high level of feeling worthless.

☞ **You keep the "real you" hidden from the outside world because you believe it makes you unworthy**: You have become very good at displaying a particular personality when you are around others, but it is not who you really are because you feel the real you is not good enough.

☞ **You always give in to others and are a people-pleaser**: Due to your need to be accepted by everyone, you tend to be a yes-person or people-pleaser. Even if you do not want to do something, you will because you do not want anyone to like you.

☞ **You constantly assess yourself against the best attributes of others**: You will always compare yourself to other people, regardless of what they are doing.

☞ **Social media makes you feel inferior**: Because everyone else on social media appears to be happier or more successful than you, social media can be depressing for you.

What Causes Someone to Suffer From an Inferiority Complex?

During childhood, feelings of inferiority are frequently common. You are developing and discovering who you are, so these feelings will occur. These minor feelings of inferiority come naturally to children as a means of helping them develop into high-functioning adults during their formative years. When given the right support to overcome obstacles, children can learn to embrace life's challenges and get over feelings of inadequacy and shame over facing hardship. But occasionally, whether because of trauma, abuse, or physical or mental impairment, these feelings of inferiority grow too strong and continue to persist into adulthood in dangerous ways. Children who experience physical or emotional abuse, particularly as a form of discipline for perceived inadequacies, may internalize these feelings and develop low self-esteem. When children are not given affection from a parent or from an adult that they care for. Sometimes, that authority figure may even view the child as unworthy of their time or affection or they may be attempting to teach the child to be tough. And in some cases, they are physically and/or emotionally unavailable. Children who experience this attempt to earn affection by achieving things.

So, they will study twice as hard as their classmates to be at the top of their class or train twice as hard to be the top player on the team. In order to get some form of recognition, attention, and/ or affection from their parents or caregivers. However, when they are still not given any form of affection for their accomplishments, feelings of inferiority and inadequacy are born. In some cases, children who experience this will also "act out" because they feel that if their accomplishments got them nothing, they feel tantrums and bad behavior will get some form of attention or reaction. Males are more prone to developing inferiority complexes than women, frequently due to a social phenomenon known as "toxic masculinity," which tends to make men believe that in order to be appropriately masculine, they must suppress their natural emotional reactions and become psychologically and economically superior to other men. In romantic partnerships, men are also more likely to feel inadequate, especially when comparing themselves with their partner's previous connections or, in some cases, if their partner is more successful than them.

Other possibilities include:

☞ **Comparing yourself to others**: For some people, social media might result in unhealthful comparisons. Remember that many Instagram photos are expertly taken, cropped, and filtered; this might give the impression that everyone there is more attractive than you and leads a lavish lifestyle. However, social media is not real life; all you see is a carefully chosen and heavily edited portion of other people's experiences. It goes beyond social media as well. Every day, the media as a whole—and advertising in particular—presents us with impossibly beautiful visuals. Additionally, if you just concentrate on other people's positive traits, you can compare yourself negatively to them.

☞ **Feeling like a failure**: This is a thought and behavior pattern that originated in early childhood. It might come from a parent who is often criticizing you or not giving you any attention, as stated above, and it can cause self-destructive behavior. You give up striving because you believe that you will never measure up to the expectations of your friends or the standards set by your parents, and your accomplishments start to become self-fulfilling.

☞ **Social isolation**: Do you think or feel as if you don't belong? This can hinder you since it incorrectly creates the impression that you are inherently inferior and/or different from other people. It is possible that you were raised with the impression that your family stood apart from the others. You might have felt less than your peers as a child. This will result in you keeping to yourself and not interacting with others.

☞ **Feelings of defectiveness**: If you believe that there is anything about you that is fundamentally faulty, inferior, or otherwise incorrect, you may want to avoid placing yourself in circumstances where you could face criticism or judgment. It is possible that you internalized your parents' frequent self-deprecation when you were growing up. Or perhaps your parents were strict achievers who made you feel like you were never good enough while you were growing up. Or perhaps you felt as a child that you would never amount to anything in life since you did not receive enough support.

☞ **Magnification/minimization**: This type of thinking is known as a "thinking trap" since it minimizes the positive and emphasizes the negative. For instance, do you constantly draw attention to your shortcomings and minimize your strengths? And do you overlook other people's shortcomings in favor of focusing on their positive traits?

☞ **Black-and-white thinking**: The all-or-nothing thinking trap, which prevents people from seeing things as more complex, nuanced, and shaded in gray, is what leads to this kind of oversimplification.

What Are the Effects of Suffering From an Inferiority Complex?

Even as adults, as stated before, we often harbor some sense of inadequacy, particularly when we compare ourselves to those who possess exceptional talent or intelligence. Any typical and normal activity, nevertheless, has the potential to become abnormal when it is carried too far. Similar reasoning applies to inferiority complexes. A crippling or disruptive sense of inadequacy affects people with this disorder in their day-to-day functioning. An inferiority complex increases a person's propensity for risk-taking, drug and alcohol abuse, and aggressive behavior. Additionally, those who are impacted are more likely to suffer from other mental health conditions like anxiety and depression. Low self-esteem, on the other hand, is also the main indicator of an inferiority complex, to the point where some psychologists use the terms interchangeably. People who have inferiority complexes may become socially isolated due to a negative self-image because they believe they are not comparable to their peers. It could also result in feelings of helplessness or frustration with achieving objectives or the idea that reaching objectives alone will not be enough. Due to their aggressive need to prove their worth, when a person has an inferiority complex, they frequently come across as either extreme overachievers or underachievers. The latter group is a result of their propensity to give up on their objectives completely when they fail to meet their own unreasonable standards and become overwhelmed or burned out.

Superiority Complex

On the flip side of feeling superior and having a superior complex, many people who are diagnosed with a superiority complex are actually trying extremely hard to cover up their feelings of inadequacy. They often work really hard to show everyone they are better than what others think of them.

How to Overcome an Inferiority Complex

To start to combat your feelings of inferiority, try the following:

Get out of the habit of comparing yourself. If you feel bad about yourself because you are constantly scrolling on social media, try to limit the amount of time you spend on those platforms as well as the people you choose to follow. And please do not think you need to be like other people, whether those you see in the media or your own friends. Everyone has their own journey in life, and we can't truly understand the difficulties others are going through. Discover what is important to you and what you want to achieve, then concentrate on those things.

Practice gratitude. Studies indicate that an attitude of gratitude for life's blessings tends to reduce social comparisons. What are you thankful for? Get in the habit of creating a gratitude list. We all have reasons to be thankful.

Challenge your thinking. Challenging negative and unproductive thought patterns that make you feel inadequate, undeserving, and flawed is one of the best things you can do. Positive thinking has entered the chatroom! If you find it difficult to do, that counseling can assist you as well.

Give yourself a chance. Try placing yourself in settings where actual accomplishments are attainable if you find that you tend to shy away from situations where you could falter or feel unworthy. Always give yourself a chance; do not tap out of the game before even entering.

Practice mindfulness. If you find yourself dwelling on past wrongdoings or worrying about the future, mindfulness meditation can help you return to the present. Studies reveal that practicing mindfulness can improve your sense of acceptance of yourself, which can lessen feelings of inadequacy. It is also a great way to help center your mind and allow the flow of positivity.

Practice self-acceptance. Embrace your imperfections and insecurities. Nobody is perfect. And that is alright. Give yourself a break, and be patient with yourself.

Seek professional help. Nothing is wrong with receiving counseling to help you get through this. This does not make you less of a person! Sometimes, a third party is needed to help and guide you. Regardless of how much knowledge you gain from my book, some of you may need a professional to help you apply the knowledge gained and also to help you deal with underlying issues.

Mindfulness and Positivity Are on the Same Team

Sometimes, your positivity tree does not get a chance to bloom because your mind is still stuck in the past and things you could have done differently. At other times, your mind drifts to a mistake you made ten years ago, and before you know it, you are flooded with negative thoughts about being a screw-up. We cannot hit the rewind button and start over. Or change what we did; I am sure many of you could, but allowing your mind to be trapped in the *shudda cudda wudda* frame is unhealthy for you. Mindfulness keeps you in the present. Reducing stress, enhancing your physical and mental well-being, and even raising your level of happiness in life are all possible with mindfulness. By practicing mindfulness, you can begin to experience its benefits. The discipline of deliberately focusing attention on the present moment and accepting it without passing judgment is known as mindfulness. Many of you need to tap into this, as what it will do is be kind to yourself and remind you of where you are now. Your brain is not programmed to stay in the past; what it wants to do is find solutions for the situation that occurred. So trying to fix something that happened ten years ago in your mind will be chaotic and difficult for you and make you frustrated, sad, etc. All the things we have been talking about.

Benefits of Mindfulness

Listed below are some of the benefits of mindfulness.

Mindfulness improves your overall well-being. Gaining more awareness enhances the probability of you adopting a positive mindset that will lead to a fulfilling existence. Being mindful increases your ability to deal with negative situations more logically and clearly, and it helps you to become more completely engaged in activities and makes it simpler to enjoy life's small pleasures; in other words, you will not only find contentment in major things, but you will appreciate the little things as well. Many people who practice mindfulness discover that by keeping their attention on the present, they are less likely to become mired in regrets about the past or fears about the future, they are less consumed with thoughts of achievement and self-worth, and they are better able to build meaningful connections with others.

Mindfulness improves your physical health. In case the discovery of enhanced well-being is insufficient motivation for you, studies have found that practicing mindfulness can have several positive effects on a person's physical health. Relieving stress, treating heart disease, lowering blood pressure, reducing chronic pain, enhancing sleep, and easing gastrointestinal issues are all possible through practicing mindfulness.

Mindfulness improves mental health. Recently, mindfulness meditation has gained popularity among psychotherapists as a crucial component of treating a variety of issues, such as obsessive-compulsive disorder, depression, substance misuse, eating disorders, marital problems, anxiety-related conditions, and couples disputes (*Benefits of mindfulness,* 2023).

Mindfulness Techniques

Although there are various approaches to practicing mindfulness, the objective of all mindfulness techniques is for you to intentionally pay attention to your thoughts and sensations without passing judgment on yourself in order to reach a state of attentiveness, focus, and calmness. This enables your mind to return to the here and now. Every mindfulness practice is a form of meditation.

☞ **Basic mindfulness meditation**: Sit still and pay attention to how you naturally breathe or repeat a word in your mind. Let thoughts come and go without deciding if they are good or bad, and then go back to focusing on your breath or a word you repeat to yourself.

☞ **Body sensations**: Pay attention to small physical sensations like an itch or tingling sensation. Do not make any judgments about them and allow them to go away on their own. Pay attention to each part of your body, starting from the top of your head and moving down to your toes.

☞ **Sensory**: Observe the sensations of taste, smell, sight, and sound. Label them by sight, sound, smell, taste, or touch without any form of judgment, and then release them.

☞ **Emotions**: It's okay to have feelings without worrying about what others might think. Try to calmly and slowly label your feelings, like happiness, anger, or frustration. Do not judge the emotions or yourself; simply acknowledge them and then release them.

☞ **Urge surfing**: Deal with strong desires (for addictive substances, food, or actions) and release them. Pay attention to how your body feels when you start to crave something. Instead of hoping that your strong desire will disappear, have confidence that it will eventually decrease.

Learn to Practice Acceptance

Above all, practicing mindfulness means learning to accept whatever comes into your awareness at any given time. It entails treating yourself with kindness and forgiveness. Here are a few other pointers to remember:

1. **Redirect with gentleness**: If you find your thoughts straying into criticism, planning, or daydreaming, gently bring them back to the sensations of the here and now.

2. **Continue trying**: Just start over if you end up missing your scheduled meditation session.

It gets simpler to accept whatever comes your way for the rest of the day when you practice embracing your experience during meditation.

Chapter 4

Creating Your Own Happiness

All of us have a higher chance of increasing our chances of happiness and fulfillment when we take the time and start to concentrate on the positive aspects of our lives. This is why adopting a positive mindset is a great contribution to your life. What this method entails is actively looking for the positive aspects of your life, particularly in the face of difficulties or disappointments. It is crucial to keep in mind that happiness is more than just the absence of bad feelings; it also involves the existence of good ones, meaning sometimes the simple things are overlooked because your mind is only focused on what is wrong at the moment. Nothing is wrong with having those moments, but as I have stated before, what I do not want is for you to be so focused on them that you miss out on other things and get overwhelmed with distress. You can produce more happy feelings by developing an optimistic outlook. And everyone benefits directly from that positivity in terms of increased fulfillment and happiness. This is not going to happen immediately; you are going to need to take time and apply certain things to your daily life. A very strong and great way to take time to develop your positive mindset is to practice gratitude. This is something that many of us ignore, as we can get caught up with the way things are not flowing well in our lives right now. What gratitude entails is consciously valuing the good things in your life and reflecting on what you have to be grateful for. You will end up fostering a more optimistic mindset and living a happier life when you put more emphasis on what you have than what you lack.

Here are some simple methods for developing gratitude and making it a part of your life:

- ☞ **Write thank-you notes to people who have impacted your life in a positive way**: Believe it or not, a simple "thank you" goes a long way. People who have done things for you without expecting anything in return but did it out of the kindness of their hearts appreciate thank-you notes. They do not have to be a long essay, just kind words from your heart expressing your thankfulness for what they have done. By taking the time to give attention and concentrating on your relationships, you can improve the bonds you share, and you can pay it forward by spreading happiness!

- ☞ **Keep a gratitude jar**: This may sound corny, but believe me, it is useful. What this entails is that you are just placing little notes about the various positive things that happened to you each day, mixed with things that you are grateful for. You could write that you were thankful that your sibling stopped by with dinner because you did not get a chance to head to the supermarket, and you were concerned about what you were going to eat. Just anything at all that has been linked to good vibes and gratitude. At the end of the year, open your gratitude jar, take a moment, and reflect on all the positive things that occurred to you during the year. It will be a humbling experience and also make you feel content and grateful.

☞ **Practice gratitude in difficult situations**: This, I know, will be a challenge. I myself had a bit of a challenge practicing this. But I found that when I was practicing it, it was, in fact, useful and very beneficial to me. So what I am saying to you is this: Not because it is a challenge, you should not try it. I am here to challenge you and help you shift your mindset. Many times, we throw in the towel before even attempting. I am here to let you know that there is value in attempting. When dealing with a difficult issue, remember to be grateful for all of your blessings, no matter how miniscule they may appear. It is difficult, but it can be done, and you can do it. For instance, you could be appreciative of a friend's or relative's assistance during a difficult situation; they could be the ones to help you out emotionally and/or financially. Or expressing gratitude for the chance to develop and learn from a traumatic event. Many of us have developed resilience and gained strength from a harrowing experience, and even though it seems a bit gloomy, it is truthful.

☞ **Practice gratitude in your daily routine**: Gratitude should be a part of your day-to-day life. For example, being thankful that you have a bed to sleep on and inside a space and not sleeping outside on the street, or, during a meal, taking time to be thankful that you have a meal that you are eating.

What I want you all to keep in mind is that by including appreciation in your everyday life, you will end up developing a more optimistic outlook on life. By focusing on fulfillment and creating your own happiness, you can be grateful for what you already have.

Create Your Own Happiness by Surrounding Yourself With Positivity

You have to become more mindful of what you read, watch, and surround yourself with as you embark on your positivity journey. What you digest daily and who you socialize with can prove to be a roadblock if you are not careful. To cultivate a positive mindset, you must spend time with uplifting friends and/or family members, coworkers, etc. Make a conscious effort to minimize the time you spend with people who are emotionally draining, only speak about negative things, shut down your ideas, or make you feel you lack the capability to achieve certain things, e.g., starting your own business. They are not providing you with positive feedback; what they are doing is dragging you down. Make it a habit to start listening to uplifting music, podcasts, or reading motivational books (like mine) or articles. You can create a supportive environment for your objectives and dreams by surrounding yourself with optimism.

Here are a few ways that you can surround yourself with positive influences:

- **You can find a mentor or role model**: Having a mentor or role model in your life can be a very effective way to surround yourself with positive energy. Many of you may shy away from this approach because you are afraid of how it will appear to others. Well, I want you to get that out of your head. It is not about others; it is about you and your growth, so throw those thoughts in the trash. Find someone who exemplifies the virtues and characteristics you respect, and make an effort to take inspiration from them. You got this!

☞ **Join a positive community**: Yes, these communities do exist! This is another excellent way to surround yourself with positivity by joining a group of like-minded individuals. Attend a workshop or seminar, sign up for a local club or group, or take part in an online community. Participate in activities with others who want to see good things happen.

☞ **Limit exposure to negativity**: On your path of positivity, you must limit negativity from your existence. Think about it: You are trying to have positive vibes, but the negative energy is at the same level. Positivity has to be dominant once too many negative thoughts exist. They will dominate your thoughts and cast a shadow on your positivity tree, blocking sunlight from it. This is why limiting your exposure to negativity is crucial. So, how do you limit negativity in your life? It may involve limiting the amount of time you spend on social media and not spending too much time reading and/or watching countless videos of murder, amongst other things. Now, I am not saying to be out of touch and not know what is happening in your country; what I am saying is that sometimes some of you spend hours reading gruesome stories, and then it interrupts your sleep patterns and floods you with high levels of sadness and depression. Also, as I stated above, limit who you socialize with; some people are just too much, and this will require you to set some boundaries with them as they really bring too much negativity into your space. It is tiring.

☞ **Practice positive self-talk**: You already know I am all for this! Get into the habit of practicing positive self-talk. Remember, you are to be focusing on your strengths; drink that positivity lemonade.

You establish an uplifting atmosphere for yourself by associating with positive people. And you will be able to develop a more optimistic outlook on life with the support of that positively charged environment.

Create Your Own Happiness by Ensuring That You Take Care of Yourself

Self-care is a must! There is no way around it; I could not be talking about positivity and creating happiness and not include how important it is that you take care of your body. Your mental and physical well-being should be a top priority. This requires you to have a nutritious diet, exercise on a regular basis, have moments to yourself when you just sit and unwind, and take time to rejuvenate. You will find that you will handle obstacles better when you take care of your body and mind, and you tend to generate more happy feelings when your body and mind are rested and taken care of.

Here are a few ways that you can take care of your physiological and psychological health:

☞ **Get in the habit of taking breaks and recharging**: Taking pauses during the day to rejuvenate is crucial. Do something euphoric, like go for a stroll outside and enjoy nature or practice mindfulness.

☞ **Set boundaries**: An essential component of self-care also includes setting boundaries. Not just with negative people but overall. Developing a positive work-life balance is essential so that you do not end up burning out or feeling drained. Learning to say no to things that do not fit with your priorities or values is an excellent example. No is not a bad or offensive word.

☞ **Take time and connect with others**: Developing and maintaining healthy interpersonal interactions is another crucial aspect of self-care. Anxiety and tension can be decreased by hanging out with friends and family, joining a cause, or engaging in activities that you find fulfilling.

☞ **Get enough sleep**: Sleep is fundamental. There is no going around this. I know I am not the only one who gets moody and easily irritated when I have not gotten enough rest. This is why I made sleep a priority. Getting enough sleep is good for you not only psychologically but physiologically as well. Try to aim for seven to eight hours of sleep each night. Try and develop a bedtime routine, so if you desire to be sleeping by 10 p.m. Do not wait until 10 p.m. to get in bed, as you will probably fall asleep by 10:30 p.m.

If the aim is for 10 p.m., make your way to your bedroom by 9:30 p.m. or 9:45 p.m. at the latest. Turn off apps that will be tempting for you to watch and set rain sounds or white noise in the background (if that works for you). Ensure your alarm is set and drift off in sleep land.

☞ **Practice self-compassion**: This is a must, guys! Practicing self-compassion is what will help you along your positivity journey as you get into the habit of taking care of yourself. I have been stressing this point: That you must be kind and patient with yourself, and I am not saying it just because I am trying to add to my word count. I am saying it because I really want you all to do it. Many of you forget to be kind to yourself. It is easy for you to do it for others, but you neglect to do it for yourself. Practice treating yourself with the same level of empathy and compassion that you would do for a friend, partner, family member, and/or child.

You lay the groundwork for a happier and more satisfying life by making self-care for your psychological and physiological well-being a priority. Always keep in mind that you are your valuable possession and that taking care of yourself is essential to achieving your goals.

Practice Mindfulness

Now, you see why I said that mindfulness and positivity are on the same team. Mindfulness, as I have mentioned in Chapter 4, helps to keep you in the present and is a great tool to use as you embark on your positivity journey. It will help you be more self-aware and aware of your thoughts and how to channel them in a constructive and useful way. Meditation, yoga, practicing breathing, and keeping your thoughts in the present are a few ways that you can practice this very useful and effective tool. Here are a few other ways that you can practice mindfulness that will help you create your own happiness and be more positive:

- ☞ **Practice mindful eating**: Increasing awareness of your eating habits is another approach to engaging in mindfulness exercises. Savor every bite of your food, taking in all of its flavors, textures, and aromas. You may make healthier decisions and enjoy your meals more if you put this into practice. You also find that you will be eating slower, which is a good thing.

- ☞ **Practice mindfulness in nature**: One of the most effective ways to develop mindfulness is to spend time in nature. Go for a hike or a stroll in a park to completely appreciate the beauty of nature. You will feel more rooted and in the moment when you are in nature.

- ☞ **Practice loving-kindness meditation**: Warm-heartedness meditation involves sending good vibes and well-wishes to yourself and other people. It will aid you in developing more empathy and compassion, and you will develop a stronger sense of community.

Increasing your awareness can help you be more present throughout the day. This behavior can help you become more conscious of your feelings and thoughts. It is especially useful in problem-solving, which is great for you. You will find that you react to things in a more constructive and positive manner, which will help you develop a more optimistic outlook on life. Keep in mind that mindfulness is a method of consistent practice that requires patience and dedication.

Setting Achievable Goals

Many times, people get discouraged or do not stick to the goals they set because they are unrealistic and unachievable. Due to this negativity, it enters the chat room and sends a barrage of negative messages, making you feel as if you cannot do anything or are not smart enough, which is all false news. A strong strategy for developing a positive outlook is to set attainable goals. Setting challenging but feasible goals gives you a sense of direction and purpose. And you will feel proud of yourself after reaching those goals. You will notice a significant increase in your sense of self-worth and confidence. Here are some strategies for creating objectives that are doable for you:

☞ **Take time to dissect massive goals**: Try dividing your significant, overwhelming goals into smaller, more achievable ones. This provides opportunities to recognize your accomplishments along your route and helps keep you motivated and focused.

☞ **Jot down your objectives**: Setting down your objectives on paper will help you make them more concrete and tangible in your thoughts. To help you stay on track, list your desired outcomes somewhere you can see them and look at them frequently.

☞ **Share your goals with others**: When there are people around you whom you trust, nothing is wrong with sharing your goals with them. Do not think that you are being a burden to them. Sometimes, you are going to need a little push along the way. Holding yourself accountable can be achieved by sharing what you want to accomplish with loved ones or friends. They will already be aware of your goals and intent when you require assistance. Additionally, they will be there to support and encourage you when you need it.

☞ **Appreciate your advancements**: Celebrating tiny victories is a good thing! No matter how tiny the progress appears, it must be celebrated. Celebrating your successes will help you stay motivated and confident while you work toward your goals.

☞ **Be flexible**: Yes, you may have made a plan that is achievable, but also remember that things happen. Being adaptable and modifying your goals when necessary is crucial. Do not get too rigid and feel as if there is only one way. Your goal may end up becoming much more difficult than you imagined due to unforeseen changes in conditions. To keep motivated and on track, be willing to modify your goals as needed and discover new strategies.

You can give your life direction and purpose and maintain motivation by defining and achieving realistic objectives for yourself. Recognize that it is critical to exercise patience, perseverance, and appreciation for each step of the journey. With enough time and work, you may accomplish your goals and build a more peaceful and positive life.

Failure Is a Life Lesson, Not a Tragedy

Failure is a part of life. It happens to everybody. The thing is, failure can teach you important lessons. Rather than criticizing yourself for past mistakes, use them as chances for personal improvement. Consider the lessons you can take away from them and how you might apply those lessons to perform better in the future. Here are some ways you can learn from failure:

- **Consider what went awry**: Think about what went wrong and why for a while. Be truthful and recognize any common patterns or reoccurring problems that may be causing your shortcomings. When doing this, please do not practice marinating in the situation and what you could have done differently, as that will not be productive and helpful. Approach it like a case study: examine, get the data, discover the issues, and make adjustments.

- **Seek feedback from others**: Now, when you are practicing this approach, please do it with an open mind and not get defensive. Asking someone's feedback is good as they can be more objective and point out things that you missed, which will help you gain knowledge and help you avoid making the same mistake again. Seeking advice from a mentor (see why nothing is wrong with having a mentor?) or life coach, or getting an honest assessment from a friend or coworker might help you look at issues from a new angle.

☞ **Reframe your mindset towards failure**: You are a marvelously and exquisitely made human being, and like all humans, you will make mistakes and fail. Even when you are trying your best, failure can occur because humans are not meant to be perfect. Try to consider failure as a normal and essential part of the learning process rather than something negative and horrible. Accepting failure as an opportunity for learning can help you adopt a growth-driven and optimistic mindset.

Gaining knowledge from failures makes you more resilient and skilled at overcoming adversity. Making errors is okay, and failing is a necessary component of learning. Using setbacks as teaching moments might help you develop a more optimistic and growth-focused perspective. You will be more able to develop a positive outlook and build your own happiness by implementing these doable suggestions into your everyday routine. It is something that you can do to block and delete negativity from the chat room. Recognize that although the process requires time and work, the benefits are worthwhile. You matter, so take some time and put in the work. It is possible to design a joyful and meaningful life by emphasizing self-care, appreciation, and optimism. And now is the best moment of all to get started! Discover doable strategies for developing a good outlook and producing your own happiness. To live a more fulfilled life, discover the value of self-care, mindfulness, gratitude, attainable goals, and gaining insight from failures.

Chapter "Good Will"

Helping others without expectation of anything in return has been proven to lead to increased happiness and satisfaction in life.

I would love to give you the chance to experience that same feeling during your reading or listening experience today...

All it takes is a few moments of your time to answer one simple question:

If so, I have a small request for you.

If you've found value in your reading or listening experience today, I humbly ask that you take a brief moment right now to leave an honest review of this book. It won't cost you anything but 30 seconds of your time—just a few seconds to share your thoughts with others.

Your voice can go a long way in helping someone else find the same inspiration and knowledge that you have.

Are you familiar with leaving a review for an Audible, Kindle, or e-reader book? If so, it's simple:

If you're on **Audible**: just hit the three dots in the top right of your device, click rate & review, then leave a few sentences about the book along with your star rating.

If you're reading on **Kindle** or an e-reader, simply scroll to the last page of the book and swipe up—the review should prompt from there.

If you're on a **Paperback** or any other physical format of this book, you can find the book page on Amazon (or wherever you bought this) and leave your review right there.

Chapter 5

Letting Go of the Worry Bug

At some point in our lives, we worry about something, whether it is a test result, final exam grades, getting into university, getting a job, etc. We will have some moments in our lives where we find ourselves worrying. However, excessive worrying tends to make us more distressed and stressed out. The worry bug starts off as tiny as an ant, and the more we worry, the more it grows and gains strength, and it moves from the size of an ant to the size of an elephant. Now, it has taken up all the room in your mind and makes it almost impossible to function like a normal adult. So, what causes us to worry? Finding the source of your worries is one of the most important aspects of figuring out how to cease worrying. As stated before, worrying is a natural aspect of human evolution. According to biology, our central nervous system frequently worries in response to stress and anxiety. When this occurs, the first thing you should do is consider what is precisely making you anxious so that you can stop worrying. A certain amount of worry can be constructive since it motivates us to solve current and actual issues. Even so, persistent concern over uncontrollable events can have a negative effect on your mental health. However, there is light at the end of the tunnel, as there are numerous techniques that exist to teach us how to reduce stress, quit worrying, and begin thriving.

Are You Worrying Too Much?

If you have brief moments of anxiety or an anxious thought, then there is probably no need to worry about your mental health or emotional stability. On the other hand, persistent worry may indicate a more serious condition, such as an anxiety disorder. Physical symptoms such as tightness in the muscles, sleeplessness or bad sleeping habits, back discomfort, stomach pain, and panic episodes can result from this kind of stress. Is persistent worry and anxiety starting to get in the way of your relationships, job, or day-to-day activities? If so, now is the moment to really commit to learning how to quit worrying.

Why Is It That You Worry So Much?

We are all different; therefore, what I may be worried about and that could cause me total distress could be totally different from you. This is why you should not compare yourself to others; you may feel your issues are minuscule when they probably are not, and the worry bug begins to take over your life. This is why there are some people who end up with persistent anxiety. Something will occur at some point that will make us worry, whether it is taking on a challenging career or being a parent for the first time. Think about and assess your self-awareness to determine certain things that cause high levels of worry in your life.

Think about whether any of the situations listed below cause your anxiety and fuel your worry bug:

- ☞ An overly demanding workplace

- ☞ Dealing with a toxic relationship

☞ Life-changing events in life, like having a kid, getting divorced, or moving to another country

☞ Having trouble making ends meet, losing your job, or saving for a large purchase (like a home or a car)

☞ Conflict in relationships with friends, family, or other people

☞ Physical health problems or issues

☞ Ordinary annoyances like house maintenance or gridlock

☞ An excessive number of societal duties, responsibilities, or commitments

☞ Insufficient time to engage in hobbies and self-care activities

☞ To effectively handle the tension that accompanies these circumstances, one must acquire techniques for ceasing to worry and beginning to live.

Ways to Stop Worrying

Here are some ways that you can stop worrying, regain control of your mind, and get rid of the worry bug.

1. **Practicing mindfulness and meditation**: Here comes mindfulness and meditation again! When I say it can come in handy in all aspects, I mean it. It could be difficult for you to focus on anything else when you are anxious. On the other hand, it is unhealthy to dwell on unfavorable ideas repeatedly. This will keep your mind trapped. This is not what I want for any of you. Sitting still and decluttering your thoughts in a

quiet area can help you feel better when you notice that your focus is flagging. Practicing mindfulness and meditation can help you become less focused on negative thoughts, reduce anxiety, and promote calmness, which diminishes worrying. With practice, meditation can also assist you with keeping things flowing, which lets you easily cross things off your to-do list and concentrate on your top objectives. Your life can genuinely change when you focus on the present and take your time.

2. **Sharing your fears with supportive friends and family**: For those of you who suffer from chronic worry, you would be surprised at how easily it is to lose yourself in your thoughts and unintentionally isolate yourself from your friends and family members. Even in moments when you want to withdraw, interacting with people can have a profound impact on your emotional health. Maintaining perspective can be aided by discussing the cause of your stress, anxiety, or concern with a family member or friend. Trying to keep everything to yourself and/or trying to deal with everything alone can add to your state of worry and stress. Therefore, speaking with understanding friends or family can help you see things differently and is a great way to put an end to your worries.

3. **Focus on what you are grateful for**: Gratitude is a must. Our brain is primed to seek out more unpleasant thoughts as soon as we fixate on one. On the other hand, training your mind to find benefits instead of worries can be achieved by practicing

gratitude. Learning to change your negative ideas can be a terrific strategy to quit worrying, even though it could take some practice. Look back at all the gems I left with you in Chapter 6 in regards to practicing gratitude to aid you here.

4. **Keeping a daily emotional journal**: This is actually a good technique to practice. When we ignore the early warning indications of worry and allow it to worsen over time (the worry bug will start to grow and gain strength, remember?) Maintaining your mental well-being and controlling your anxiety require frequent self-check-ins. By the time you find yourself in a worry loop, you will no longer feel emotionally involved. You can actively manage stress and pinpoint certain patterns before your emotions get out of control by keeping an emotional journal. It gets simpler to recognize when you are beginning to worry as you get more comfortable writing down your feelings and discussing your ideas in your journal. In the end, worrying less will make you feel better and keep your attention on the things that are most important to you.

5. **Distinguish between what you can control and what you cannot control**: Most of the time, we worry about things we have zero control over. Typically, worrying is directed toward some issue that has to be resolved, drawing our attention away from the here and now and onto "what if." A common misconception is that the more time you spend worrying about an issue, the easier it is to discover a solution. But has that ever worked for any of you? If

you have a job interview, do your due diligence and research all you can about the business, and make sure that you are prepared. This will help with feelings of nervousness. But at the end of the day, you will still have no control over whether they hire you or not, so do not allow the worry bug to gain any strength here.

6. **Taking positive action**: One of the best ways to manage your stress and break the habit of worrying is to do something you truly enjoy. Taking a positive approach helps you release excess energy and divert your attention from what is worrying you. You may immediately change your mindset and quit worrying by concentrating on something that makes you feel happy. Here are some strong, constructive steps you can take right now:

   ☞ Take a stroll while you're enjoying your favorite podcast.

   ☞ Use your creativity to paint or work on an endeavor; your favorite store's craft section certainly has many kits with everything you need.

   ☞ Eat a tasty snack and watch your favorite show on Netflix.

   ☞ Play your favorite music while you clean your house or do the dishes.

   ☞ Ultimately, one of the most effective ways to learn how to quit worrying is to engage in a recreational activity you genuinely enjoy.

Stop Overthinking and Enjoy Your Life

I know I do not have to tell you how exhausting overthinking is. When you overthink, your mind races with ideas and you become stationary, unable to take any more action. In addition, you begin to generate odd concepts that are in complete opposition to one another. "I'm so excited to go on this date" transforms into "I wonder if they liked me" and then morphs into "Oh no, I should not have said that joke! I am so stupid! They are definitely not going to ask me out again." You begin to worry about things that may or may not occur and begin to blame yourself for stuff you failed to do. Thinking about something excessively or for an extended period of time is known as overthinking. It's an energy-sapping feeling that I am quite familiar with, and I had to put some things into practice to rid myself of it. Actually, a study indicates that thinking too much causes stress, lowers creativity, impairs judgment, and takes away your ability to make decisions. Thankfully, overthinking can be managed in a few different ways. These don't happen instantly; some need time to develop, while others can be put into practice right away.

However, each of them calls for deliberate effort on your part:

☞ **Change the narrative you are telling yourself**: If you practice telling yourself every day that "I can never get work to on time, I am more of a night person than a morning person!" What will happen is that you will end up being that person who is always running late for work, which will leave you panicky and in a constant state of rush. You eventually start to believe and become what you tell yourself and how you consistently define yourself. Our identity and fundamental values are the source of everything we do and go through in life.

☞ **Release yourself from the past**: You gotta let it go, guys! (Cue the theme song from the movie Frozen) Overthinkers have the tendency to dwell on the past. When this happens, they are focusing their energy on the hypothetical scenarios "I wish" and "I should have." However, that energy is taking you out of the here and now. The lessons, meanings, and perspectives you draw from the past can be altered, but the past itself cannot be changed; it is just not possible. You release yourself from the burden of the past when you embrace it for what it was. Then, you will be able to release yourself from the weight, errors, and resentment of the past that are preventing you from acting in the present. You need to continuously practice letting go of the past because it is so easy to relapse into an obsessive habit. This is critical because it frees up the brain space that overanalyzing has taken up.

☞ **Focus on what you can control**: It is not helpful to worry about how you are going to pay the bills if you are having financial difficulties. A helpful exercise is to examine your spending habits and ask yourself, "What can I cut back on or remove from my bills?" Next, ask yourself, "What extra income sources can I create?" This is how you focus on the things that you can control instead of the things that you can't.

Chapter 6

People Pleasing Is a No-No

When you find yourself stuck in the habit of trying to always please people and wanting to get everyone to like you, you will find that negativity will become more prevalent in your life. This negativity will not only affect you but also others around you. Think about it for a minute. Oftentimes, people who are people-pleasers wear masks, and yes, I said masks. Because you switch up your personality with different groups and/or persons. You are living under a constant façade. This is very exhausting and stressful because it will feed the worry bug and heighten your anxiety levels. Also, due to the fact that you are a people-pleaser, you tend to say yes to people on a regular basis, even when you do not want to, because you fear these people and/or a specific person will not like you. You say yes, yes. But this comes with a price because you will find that people will take advantage of you. Also, you will feel like an imposter in your own body because what you truly want is not aligned with your true self. You also live in constant fear that these people will one day see through the façade, and that scares you. You feel as if they will be disgusted with the fact that you pretended for as long as you did. Think about all of that, and you see why people-pleasing is a no, no. It is so much more work to pretend than to be yourself. There is a group of people that you will vibe with, who will be a great match for you, and who will appreciate you for you. Also, living your life for people does not bring any form of contentment. Those of you who are struggling with this may be wondering how you can change this behavior. You have known it for so long, but you are ready to change. Also, people-pleasing gets in the way of your positivity journey.

It allows negativity to dominate, and we are not about that life. Listed below are steps that will help you stop this behavior and get you on the path to change:

1. **Recognize that, regardless of what you do, some individuals do not care about you or what you do**: Newsflash, there are some people who cannot be pleased, so you are stressing yourself out for no reason. It has nothing to do with you; it has nothing to do with what you do or do not do. It is about them. They could be going through their own personal battles and have tapped out of socializing, or they could be projecting their feelings of distress and annoyance onto those around them. They could be dealing with financial difficulties, marital problems, etc. You can begin to break free from this destructive and ineffectual behavior by realizing that no matter what you do, you will never be able to win over everyone's approval or avoid conflict.

2. **You are going to have to learn how to say no**: When you find yourself with the title of people-pleaser, saying no becomes the most difficult thing for you to do. However, it is essential for your own well-being, stress tolerance, and leading the life you really desire. Remember, we touched on this before,

but I feel that I have to stress this point. If the person is being forceful, stand your ground and state what you are feeling. There are some people who have an aggressive way of speaking and are asking for things, and that can be intimidating. However, you are an adult and do let that approach shift from the fact that you do not want to do what they are asking you to do or go where they are inviting you. Furthermore, you can say that you do not think this offer is a suitable fit for your life at this time. Or you can simply say that you are too busy to fulfill their requests. Expressing your true feelings to someone can make it easier for them to see things from your perspective. Also, it is far more difficult to argue against your feelings than your thoughts.

3. **Develop coping mechanisms for insults and criticism**: The fear of someone commenting about you in a negative way or receiving any form of criticism tends to be the reason some of you end up becoming people pleasers. Let me guide you through this so that this fear will no longer hold you hostage. Tips to help you handle criticism and insults are:

   ☞ **Take a brief moment before you reply**: If you received an email that was harsh and/ or insulting as you sit in front of your laptop, staring at your inbox, take a few deep breaths. You will lessen your chances of getting angry with yourself, making a mistake in your response, or chasing the person down for approval. It is always a good idea to take a moment to compose yourself before responding. This is where practicing mindfulness meditation will be very helpful.

☞ **You do not have to reply to all the negative messages you may get via email, social media, or in person**: Saying nothing and moving on are also options. I mean, this is easier said than done, but you can do it. Although this obviously doesn't work in every circumstance, it's vital to keep in mind that you do occasionally have this option. Also, there are some people who feed off getting people riled up, so please do not give them any fuel.

☞ **It is okay to disagree**: You do not always need everyone to see the point you are trying to make or reach a common ground. Sometimes it is okay to agree to disagree and keep it moving. Once you start to adopt this concept and viewpoint, you will notice that your life will start to get lighter and simpler.

☞ **Set boundaries for yourself and stick to them**: Saying no to yourself and establishing solid boundaries will eventually make it simpler to extend the same courtesy to other people. Establishing limits can also aid in improving your attention to the things that are most important to you.

1. **Strengthen your self-esteem**: Why is this significant? You will respect yourself and your time and energy more if you have a self-esteem toolbox full of beneficial habits. As a result, saying no when necessary will come more naturally to you. Negative remarks and criticism won't have the same effect on you. You will not worry as much about winning people's approval all the time. Due to the fact that you no longer rely as much on what other people may think or say, you now value and appreciate yourself more.

2. **Keep your focus on what you want out of your life**: No will no longer be a bad word, and you will cease pleasing people because you know what is most vital to you, and your attention will be there more frequently. Your needs and wants are currently taking up the majority of your time and attention. You will no longer be just aimlessly cruising along, which is fantastic because it's easy to get sucked into the trap of doing what other people want when you lack concentration.

Ways to Stop People Pleasing Practically

It may take some time to pinpoint exactly what you truly want. However, this is a good place to start. What are the three most significant things in your life at this moment? It might be the business you are starting. Your family, your profession, your overall well-being, your pet, taking up a new hobby, sports, enhancing your social circle, or decluttering your house—whatever they are, make sure you consider them and jot down the top three significant things in your life. There is no right or wrong answer; these are your priorities, and they have nothing to do with anyone else. After you have created your list, proceed to create reminders. Write down your top three most important things on a small piece of paper. And place it in a space where you see it daily. It will keep you centered on yourself and not let your mind drift and get caught up in thinking about who you plan on impressing.

Valuing Yourself Should Be a Top Priority: Defining Self-Value and Self-Worth

It is important to highlight self-value and self-worth, even though my main goal is centered around getting people who are struggling with self-value to make this a part of their lives. Lacking self-value will hinder you from tapping into your full potential and will also prohibit your positive tree from reaching its full growth and strength. Your perception of and behavior toward yourself in your day-to-day life are greatly influenced by your sense of self-worth and self-value. Both should be used to express how much you appreciate yourself, both in words and deeds. Feeling that you are a decent person who should be treated with dignity is the foundation of self-worth. The feeling that you are kind, empathetic, and deserving of the same things in return comes naturally to someone who values themselves. Moving toward more concrete actions that develop and support your own worth is made possible when you synchronize yourself with it. Self-worth is the means by which this is accomplished. Value comes from behavior, whereas worth comes from emotion. Here is where we apply the basic principles of our self-perception. The motivation behind our ability to act in accordance with our values and to walk the walk is our sense of self-worth. This is evident in the way we interact with others and in the actions, we take to communicate the truth. Although self-worth and self-value are mutually reinforcing, they are basically sisters, so it is important to recognize their slight distinctions.

How Do These Two Terms Differ?

Self-worth is fundamental to who we are. It is how we embrace our lives and our responsibilities, and it is how we grow into human beings that are worthy. It is also plausible to contend that our choices in relationships, decisions, and life trajectories are significantly influenced by a sound sense of self-worth. Nonetheless, low self-esteem can result in harsh levels of self-criticism and a negative self-perception. Maintaining your alignment with your own worth is a function of your sense of self-value. Another way to conceptualize self-value is as an additional component of the overall concept of self-worth. There are various practical ways to value yourself, some of which I have outlined below. When you develop a sense of self-worth, you not only cultivate that worth within yourself but also radiate that energy outward to people around you, which will contribute to having a more optimistic approach to life.

Learning How to Value Yourself

- ☞ **Recognize the inner critic in your mind**: I have discussed self-talk, and I hope you understand how influential it is when it comes to the decisions you make. This is why negative self-talk must be something that you no longer partake in. That inner voice interferes with your ideas and ongoing initiatives and frequently dissuades you from believing in yourself or taking certain risks that can change your life in a good way. It keeps you in a state of fear. Your self-esteem can suffer greatly if your inner critic is allowed to run amok in your mind. You cannot develop your sense of worth when it dominates your thoughts. Recognizing your inner critic is an excellent place to start; it is not something that will switch off and never come back again. That is not possible; this will be a lifelong process. This is why mindfulness meditation and all the tools I have listed are important to practice; the more you practice them and gain control, the easier it becomes to silence that inner critic. There are so many people who do not even realize how much of a tyrant this voice has become, and they spend their entire lives listening to it to the point that they now live their lives on autopilot. Pause, acknowledge that you are in charge of all decisions, and change your focus to regain control and self-worth.

☞ **Take time and truly accept a compliment**: The next time someone says something nice to you, take a moment to observe whether you immediately return the compliment or brush it off almost immediately because you do not wish to draw any attention to yourself. Most people rarely accept kind comments from others because they are so terrified of appearing needy. Spoiler alert: The real offender here is thinking you do not deserve to receive compliments! The great thing about this is that we do not always perceive ourselves the same as other people do. Therefore, the next time someone compliments you, embrace it and thank them. You do not need to do anything else.

☞ **Be grateful to yourself for making an effort**: Everything is connected. When speaking about happiness, I spoke extensively about gratitude and how it plays an important role. With self-value, it also plays an important role. Being appreciative of your accomplishments is one way to increase your sense of self-worth. Even when you are trying your hardest, it is easy to criticize yourself and wish you had done better. However, it is important that you acknowledge even little victories. Your entire being will be thankful.

☞ **Practice forgiving yourself**: When you make a mistake, or maybe even offend someone, yes, you had a moment of failure; yes, you said something mean. But please do not let it flood your thoughts and make you feel that you are the worst person on the planet. I have to stress again that forgiving yourself is a key component at each stage of your life, and as you get in touch with a positive mindset, you will realize how essential this tool is.

☞ **Let go of comparison**: This has made its way into the chatroom again. In order to learn how to increase your self-value, you have to remember that there is no one like you. You are unique. Comparing yourself to others will cast a shadow over you that will keep you down, and that is not fitting for any of you. Focus on your own goals, dreams, talents, etc. And not focus and/or compare your life to others. Their goals and their lives have nothing to do with you.

☞ **Find different ways to serve others**: You will nurture your own sense of value and self-worth at the same time when you exercise selfless service. Providing something of yourself that is distinctly valuable and your own to others goes a long way, and I know many of you may be thinking I am talking about volunteering alone. Listen, I am all for volunteering; it is a great thing to do. However, this goes beyond simple volunteer work. Your community prospers when you give back to the world, whether it is through a particular ability you possess or just by giving your time.

☞ **Accept yourself just as you are**: Reliving the past is pointless since it has already happened, and there is nothing you can do to change it. Do not let the past hinder your progress. Thinking about the future is pointless as well because it has not yet arrived. As much as we would love to know what will happen next, we will not. Do not give yourself a headache trying to figure out if you will get married three years from now, etc. Acknowledging who you are at this precise time is the greatest gift you can give to yourself. When you are as genuine as you can be, humanity is more complete. It also gives others the bravery to follow suit. You will undoubtedly develop and alter as your life goes on. Remain in the present.

☞ **Do not settle for the bare minimum**: If you find yourself in an unhappy situation, acknowledge it and begin to consider what could bring you happiness. Anything or anyone that does not make you happy or leave you feeling fulfilled is not something you have to put up with. There is no law that surrounds that. Also, you all got great tips on creating your own happiness in Chapter 4; you got this! Also, it is a common misconception that we must compromise our happiness in order to achieve a certain goal, but let me tell you straight up, that is wrong. In life, alternatives are always available. It is up to you to think, know, and accept that the best ones are yours. Do not let anyone tell you otherwise.

☞ **When in doubt, remember your perseverance**: Unexpected events frequently arise in life. As you are all aware, you may have a straightforward plan, and out of nowhere, an unforeseen incident occurs. It can really rattle you, or it can really put you in a state of shock, and you are going to need a minute. However, thinking that you are inadequate or have failed in some way is one of the things that might undermine your sense of worth. When this occurs, consider your ultimate objective or aspiration.

Keep in mind that persistence is the never-ending source of energy you may use to keep going farther. Having tenacity is the general term that captures our essence and the essence of what it is to be human. The definition and goal of self-value are the actions we take to consciously and practically align ourselves with that worth. These kinds of steps could seem difficult and laborious. Thankfully, that is not the case at all. Shifting your perspective on how you present yourself in life gradually is necessary to start appreciating who you are. For both the broader good and for yourself, such tiny but significant adjustments can make a huge difference.

Chapter 7

How to Use Positive Thoughts to Achieve Your Goals

In this last chapter, I want those of you who have set achievable and realistic goals to use positive thoughts and actions to execute these goals. To assist you in overcoming negative thought patterns that have previously kept you from reaching your goals, I've included a number of positive thinking techniques. Select a few that you think will be most beneficial to you and make them a part of your everyday routine. Put these techniques on paper and make a mental note to stop and adopt a new perspective if you catch yourself becoming judgmental of yourself. As you get more accustomed to every new style of thinking, for instance, it will be simpler for you to learn not to accept responsibility for other people's anger and to stop apologizing.

Try including a fresh method for thinking positively on your list:

☞ **Keep away from extremes and exaggerations**: If you catch yourself saying things like "I eat way more than my friends; I eat too much" or "I will never lose weight; it is just not possible," stop yourself. This is your inner voice coming with a wild exaggeration. What you are doing is proclaiming the absolute truth about your life, and let me let you in on a little secret:

There are not that many absolutes in life. Rephrase your statement if you use absolute truth or a very elaborate exaggeration. For example, modify how you state certain things, so instead of saying, "I always eat too much," switch it to, "There was a time in my life when I would often eat too much. However, I am becoming better at controlling how much I eat now." Then, take pride in managing your concepts.

☞ **Halt negative thoughts immediately**: I have repeated this so much that hopefully, when you blink, it flashes before your eyes. It can be that simple to stop thinking negatively at times. Just by telling yourself to halt your internal self-criticism the next time it occurs! You would certainly urge someone to stop insulting other people if you witnessed them doing so, wouldn't you? Why do you allow yourself to behave in that way?

☞ **Look for that positive cloud**: We are a team of self-love and self-compassion. Show love to both yourself and other people, and instead of concentrating on your perceived flaws, highlight your positive traits. Maybe you did not have the endurance to run longer on the treadmill or do those fifty extra squats this month, but maybe you lost five pounds as a result of your dedication and hard work. Celebrate this! Perhaps attending a formal social event made you feel anxious and self-conscious, and you wished you were funnier or smiled more; however, your friends told you how much they enjoyed having you join them.

☞ **It is okay to slip up**: What is another major point I have stressed here? In case you forgot, you are a human being. You are going to mess up. That does not make you abnormal. Be patient with yourself; a mess is going to happen. Perhaps you feel guilty for giving in and eating those nachos, or perhaps you became so anxious and humiliated that you could not keep up in your aerobics class. I am here to let you know that it is okay. Everybody has weaknesses, and we all occasionally stray from the path or perform tasks less skillfully than we believe we should. Everyone has experienced humiliating moments and disappointments, including your president, favorite movie star, friends, family, and coworkers. I want to stress again that perfection is a very high, unachievable aim for human beings to reach; do not even begin or stop there. Make the ideal outcome by doing your best. Pay attention to the lessons you learned from the experience and how you may use them going forward. Refrain from dwelling on what went wrong or what ought to have been done differently. Give yourself permission to make errors, and then learn from them. Also, when you slip up, brush yourself off and try again.

☞ **Self-bullying is a big "no"**: Being bullied is horrible, and it is very traumatic. So why do it to yourself? Do not expect anything from yourself that you would not expect from others. It is admirable that you want to succeed. Nothing is wrong with having ambition and drive. However, it is a vicious cycle to punish yourself when you do not meet the expectations you set when they are at superhero level; you did not land her on the shuttle from an alien planet with superhero powers. Phrases such as "I should have" are nothing more than self-punishment after something has already occurred. We talked about the *shudda wudda cudda* stuff, so quit it. Proceed while staying in the now. It gets heavy to bring the past along for the voyage. Remember, you can succeed, and treat yourself with kindness!

☞ **Encourage yourself**: It is great when you have cheerleaders cheering for you and doing backflips for you. But you have to also practice being your own cheerleader! You have to get in the habit of cheering yourself on! Instead of thinking about what is wrong, try to give yourself more support and motivation instead of pointing out what went wrong and the mistakes you made. Offer yourself more helpful ideas instead of finding faults.

☞ **Get rid of the guilt**: It is not always your fault when things go wrong or someone has a problem. Taking accountability and saying sorry for mistakes is a very good trait, but this is only applicable if you made a mistake or may have hurt someone's feelings. You gain knowledge and continue forward. But it becomes problematic when you start feeling responsible for all the problems that occur or that you are the reason someone is upset. Many of you start almost every sentence with "I am sorry," or you may know people like that. You will end up with this high level of guilt that you carry with you for no reason. Take some time, be mindful of what you say, and do not walk around with the guilt cloud that is constantly raining on you.

☞ **Please note that you are only responsible for you**: No, I am not trying to tell you to be selfish and heartless, nor am I promoting anyone to be a self-absorbed narcissist. What I am saying is that sometimes things go wrong, and it has absolutely nothing to do with you. Therefore, you do not and should not have to take responsibility for everything that happens. Isn't that heavy? Remember, we are human beings. You have to take care of yourself. If you do not take care of yourself first, then you will be overly exhausted, among other things. Now, do not get me wrong; it is nice if you can also have a positive impact on others, but be mindful that you do not have control over their thoughts, feelings, and actions. So, you cannot take it personally if someone refuses your help or snaps at you for no reason. Being helpful is good, but you do not have to try to do everything for everyone. Again, this is placing too much weight on yourself. Let others take care of themselves and their choices. You are not in charge of making others happy. If someone asks for assistance and you can provide it, great! Just keep in mind that nobody has the power to make somebody else happy. Each person is responsible for their own emotions. Attempting to make someone feel a specific way is a pointless use of your energy.

☞ **Take accountability for your feelings**: As I mentioned before, you cannot make other people happy. Therefore, you cannot expect others to make you happy or help you feel better about yourself. Do not get angry with someone for not making you happy or making assumptions like "My face was sad; he should have known I was upset." To my knowledge, no one can read minds. Also, making assumptions is a great playground for overthinking. You all know that overthinking is just not it. Remember that you make your own decisions and create your own feelings. The way you feel can be shaped by different factors, but your emotions cannot be manipulated or compelled by them. What people think and say about you only matters if you let it matter to you. This is difficult; trust me, I know, but it can be achievable. There are many of you who are giving people way too much control over your lives. The most important thing is what you say to yourself and how you respond to others.

☞ **Remember to be kind to yourself**: It is easier for people to treat themselves in ways that they would not think twice about treating others. Do you label yourself as a loser, fat, not that talented, or unattractive? Would you characterize a friend using those terms? Probably not. So why do this to yourself? Remember that you are deserving of good treatment. Sometimes, it is good to treat yourself to something pleasant, whether it's an act of self-care (giving yourself a compliment) or a thought (treating yourself to a spa day).

☞ **Just let it go**: No, I am not going to hear that famous track from the movie Frozen again. But as you take on this new journey, I have to remind you one more time that you have to practice letting things go. You don't have to do everything for everyone or make everyone happy. Allow yourself to believe that you are doing the best you can. Rather than seeking approval from others, proactively assess your own performance and acknowledge your own positive efforts. Remind yourself instead.

☞ **Wipe the slate clean**: Do not hold onto gut-wrenching memories and negative feelings because they will make you think more negative thoughts and feel bad. Your previous actions and experiences can affect your life right now and prevent you from having a successful future if you allow them to. Imagine your mind is constantly replaying that horrible event that happened in 2010, and we are in 2023. Do you see how that leaves you stuck? Do you see how it can hinder you from reaching your true potential? You are going to need to forgive the bad things that happened in the past and continue with your life. This means letting go of any guilt or blame you have for yourself. Forgiveness is something you do for yourself; it is to help you, not for someone else. It helps you find peace and joy. Forgiving someone does not mean you agree with their behavior; doing something bad is still not right. The reason for forgiveness is to make you feel free because when you hold onto anger, it is like placing your mind in solitary confinement. If you find it difficult to forgive or forget, you can talk to a close friend or counselor about how you feel. However, it is important not to marinate on the issue too much, as it will consume and hinder your growth. It is necessary to resolve problems or challenges, but you should not allow your previous experiences to shape or control what happens in your future.

☞ **Focus on the possibilities ahead**: Steer clear of negative language and "can't" thinking. We tend to call it quits before trying by saying things like, "I can't run 1 km, so let me not bother," or "I can't ask that person on a date; I bet I am not their type." Never hesitate to ask for assistance when needed, but keep in mind that you do not want or need other people's approval to feel proud of what you have accomplished. Pay attention to your abilities. Remember all the good things you are capable of doing. Let go of the past and focus on the future in order to make changes. Tell yourself that you are concentrating on the important things that will guarantee your success and peace this time. Believe in yourself! Do not ever stop doing that.

The Positivity Journal and How It Is Beneficial for You

I mentioned that keeping a gratitude journal is a great thing to do, and I listed the benefits that come with it in terms of enhancing your positivity level and creating your own happiness. But I need to spend some time highlighting how important and beneficial keeping a positivity journal is. It is something I started practicing when I tapped into the positivity code. Writing is a very effective and powerful mechanism that many people overlook. This is why I want to encourage you to start a positivity journal. Introducing this style of writing into your life could be another great way to help shift your mindset and adopt a more optimistic outlook on life. I am not going to lie; in the beginning, I was a bit inconsistent with doing this, and I had to find ways to keep myself on track. So, I know how journaling is in the beginning. This is why many people do not take it on, or after a couple of days or a week, they stop as they find it to be mundane and start looking at it as a task and pressuring themselves as to what looks or sounds good. So, let me take some time to expound on this: You are not writing a thesis or presenting at a symposium. This is about you. Stop creating unnecessary stress in your life. Remember that being perfect is not a task achievable by mortals. It would be ideal if you truly understood the advantages so that it would help you, as it did me, to preserve and keep at it. The distinction is that you can be inspired and feel better by keeping a positive journal. It can improve your general health and well-being and is an essential component of self-care. Maintaining a positive journal is beneficial to everyone. People with anxiety disorders, including obsessive-compulsive disorder, have been shown to benefit from positive journaling.

Take into consideration the following advantages of positive journaling:

1. **Keeping a positivity journal fosters creativity**: All of you have some level of creativity. Creativity has a euphoric aspect to it. It is amazing! However, there are many people who need motivation to access their creativity, and journaling can be a helpful tool for that. When you allow yourself to be creative, it can help you feel peaceful and more centered. Why do you think people like to paint, learn to play

musical instruments, and make crafts? Your imagination can help you in many parts of life, and keeping a journal is a way to begin.

2. **It helps you release bottled-up emotions**: Being able to let go of your suppressed emotions is a necessary component of your emotional well-being. You carry a great deal of stress as you trod through this journey of life. You will always experience stress, regardless of your financial situation or place of residence. Nothing will change without stress in your life, but the kicker is how you manage it when it occurs. Keeping a journal gives you a wonderful way to release your dissatisfaction and cultivate a more optimistic outlook.

3. **Maintaining a positivity journal enhances your gratitude level**: Look at how the positivity journal and gratitude mesh well together. Your perspective will shift if you take the time to write down five things each day for which you are thankful. When you start focusing on the positive aspects of things rather than just the negative ones, your perspective will change.

4. **It will shift your mood in a good way**: Do you want to shift your mood from sullen to better? Or do you want to come out of the sadness box? Keeping a positivity journal is just what you need! Pardon me if you read that and felt as if it were being phrased for an infomercial. But on a serious note, it really can help improve your mood. When you make a list of the things that make you feel grateful, the things you want to achieve, and the good things in your life, it

will definitely make you feel different. When you focus strictly on the bad things and only the negative and constantly create these worst-case scenarios, before you know it, you will become a very pessimistic person. That may not have been your intention, but that is how potent negativity can get when it is given enough fuel. But keeping your positivity journal and learning to shift your mood to being grateful, looking at your strengths, etc. You will notice a shift in your mood; you will see life in a more positive light, and you will have a better mood.

5. **Use your positivity journal to demonstrate your development and personal progress**: Keeping your positivity journal has no right or wrong method; it can be like a roadmap. You are free to arrange your words however you choose. If your goal is to lose weight or become sober, having this journal can be very essential. You can track your starting point and follow your development. Through these writings, you can reflect on the challenges you have faced and the progress you have made. One benefit of keeping a positivity journal is that it can be quite beneficial to your mental health to witness your advancements.

6. **It can improve your quality of life**: Whatever you choose to name it, dedicating a portion of your day and practicing appreciation can make a big difference in the quality of your life. Even writing down five things each day for which you are grateful can significantly enhance your mood. You must use this time to focus on yourself and set everything else aside if you want to live an outstanding life. Locate a

cozy spot where you can sit by yourself and reflect on all the blessings in your life. Keep in mind that, as this is a positivity journal, you should emphasize the good things in your life. Some of you may be wondering: What if nothing positive occurred in my life then what? Just like with gratitude, there is always something positive. You may only link positivity to major events, and this is where I want you all to start to shift your focus and look at everything on a broader scale. There are more positive things that could have occurred, like:

- ☞ "I got an unexpected salary increase."

- ☞ "My children picked me sunflowers and made me an arts and crafts gift."

- ☞ "I had a productive day at work, and things flowed well."

- ☞ "I tried a new recipe, and my family loved it."

- ☞ "I baked a cake for the first time, and even though it had a dip in there it made it unique, and it tasted great."

- ☞ "I took my first online Spanish class today, after years of saying I would."

- ☞ "I tried yoga today and decided I would stick it out; I will keep track of it here!"

- ☞ "I went to the mall today and bought a Rick and Morty Shirt that made me laugh."

- ☞ "I took my first bicycle lesson today."

- ☞ "Today is my third day sober."

- ☞ "I watched a survival show and learned how to make fire."

- ☞ "I went camping with my friends; the fire-making lesson from that survival show was useful!"

- ☞ "I went to a swimming class today after fearing water my whole life."

- ☞ "I made it home before the rain started!"

I want to emphasize that you are free to arrange your journal any way you see fit, but the important thing is to start recording positive and happy experiences. You will appreciate the small details that make your life so special when you look back on this list in the future. Reading stuff like some of the examples listed above (but with your memories) can lift your spirits on days when it seems like life is too harsh, and you do not think you can handle it.

1. **Your positivity journal will make room for spiritual growth**: When you make an effort to keep an optimistic outlook, you learn to be thankful for each cycle you go through. Your ability to cope with difficult situations can have a big impact on your mental stress. When you accept that adversity fosters growth, it transforms your perspective on life's challenges. Many people have become aware of the need for more powerful heavenly assistance and guidance through positivity journaling and related processes.

2. **You will notice a major boost in your self-esteem**: You should definitely get into keeping a daily positivity journal to boost your self-esteem. You will find it difficult to maintain low self-esteem once you have been reminded of your value. When my positivity journal became a part of my daily life, I became more focused on my body in a positive way. I stopped obsessing about weight when I started focusing on my entries about the changes I made in my life, re: eating more healthy meals and those healthy activities that I wrote about and how I felt after doing them, and I had a more positive self-perception overall. I had a greater acceptance of people around me and myself. If it can do that for me, I know that it can do that for you.

3. **You will notice an overall improvement in relationships**: When was the last time you received recognition for your efforts at work or at home? When you were given this compliment, how did it make you feel? Although it feels great to have your accomplishments acknowledged, did you realize that it can also strengthen your bonds with others? The idea that receiving praise improves relationships seems strange. Because of this, some individuals think it proves that being grateful to others and receiving gratitude yourself fosters closer relationships. It can enhance both your romantic and professional connections.

4. **You will sleep a lot better**: Getting enough sleep is critical to maintaining your emotional health. Gratitude and positivity work hand in hand, so

practicing gratitude and writing it in your positivity and/ or gratitude journal will end up making you have an optimistic outlook on life and sleep better at night. Sleep is essential; there is nothing worse than having negative thoughts flood your mind, causing you to toss and turn just to get a few hours (if so much) of sleep. Sometimes, you may end up tossing and turning so much that by the time you are finally getting into the mode of sleep, it is time to wake up.

5. **Writing in your positivity journal enhances your psychological Well-Being**: I am rooting for your mental health! I want nothing that crowds your mental space. Your mental health will greatly benefit from your decision to adopt an optimistic outlook. When you keep a daily optimism journal, you will find that you are more upbeat about your future. Maintaining such a journal has positive effects on your physical and emotional well-being.

Things That You Should Always Track in Your Positivity Journal

Always remember to track the day's events in your positivity journal. In the beginning, you may need to use reminders to do this, but as time goes by, you will see that it will become second nature to you. Remember, whether it is a major or minor thing, it must be placed in your positivity journal. When you record what happens in your life, it will help you see what a normal day in your life is like. Also, please, when you are reading through your day, approach it in a non-judgmental way. Do not start thinking that you are boring or that your life is boring, etc.

Remember, this is your positivity journal. I promise you, no one is trying to give a low score, like a movie review. When you remember these things happening, you might want to write about how they made you feel. For example, if you took a stroll in the park one weekend, you might notice how much you loved the sun and how it looked on your skin, the sound of the birds in the trees, or how much you enjoyed how the leaves danced as the wind blew on them. Even if something seems "ordinary," it is still important because it was a part of your day. Each day you have is good, and there is always a positive aspect to it. Write down any difficulties you encounter. Make sure to write down any difficulties you experience throughout the day. Once again, events can either be large or small. Maybe someone was mean to you at the supermarket, or you could not find your house keys, and it took you an hour to locate them. No matter what difficulties you face, make sure to write them in your journal of positive thoughts.

Do not forget that you have other people to support you. Everyone has difficulties in their everyday life. Here are some common challenges that you may face at some point in life, which can be a challenge on your positivity journey:

☞ Feeling like an outsider at school.

☞ Feeling totally isolated at work and not having anyone to socialize with

☞ You are not really sure about what you want to do with your life moving forward, meaning you cannot decide which career path is suitable for you; you are indecisive about going to university; you are unsure if you should return to school as an adult; and you are trying to figure out if you should change jobs.

☞ Feeling like you cannot get a minute for yourself. Family and/or work at times can get very time-consuming, and it is not that you do not want to be around your family, but you feel as if you cannot get any "me time."

☞ Financial constraints: You are struggling to make ends meet, or you are up to your nose in debt.

☞ You stretch yourself thin. You tend to be always attending or doing something because you say yes all the time (this sounds like being a people-pleaser, what do you think?)

☞ Relationship issues with family, partners, and/or friends. You find that lately, you are in constant conflict with them, and it is stressing you out. You have had enough.

☞ You are neglecting self-care. Your whole energy is off because you are not taking care of yourself physiologically, nutritionally, or psychologically.

☞ Rolling with too many negative people. As discussed before, negative people are draining! All they do is discourage you, flood you with negativity, and stress you out.

1. **Remember the positive events of the day**: Can you tell me what good things you did to face the difficulties mentioned? I mean, there is a lot that can happen, and I just want you to really understand how things mess with your positive vibe, but the aim is to

get back on track and challenge yourself in your approach. For example, that means the cashier in the supermarket, take some deep breaths and do not give grouchy Susan your energy; smile and keep it moving. Maybe when searching for your house keys, you could have played your favorite music, I am not saying that this is the approach you will use, just giving you some food for thought. Write down the steps you took to overcome the challenges that you listed in your positivity journal.

2. **Write down the things you achieve each day in your journal, focusing on positive things**: As you think about what happened each day, try to find things you did well that made you feel good about yourself. They do not have to be major events (e.g., saving an elderly person from a burning building) to still have meaning and value. Maybe you finished reading a book that challenged your thinking skills or sorted out the sheets in your bathroom closet. Here are some other things you can write about:

   ☞ Take small actions to finish a project that you have delayed for some time or start a new project.

   ☞ Going back to the gym after not going for a long time.

   ☞ Eating nutritious food throughout the day. It's like a legit healthy day!

   ☞ Making a phone call that you were scared to make in order to connect with someone you wanted to get in touch with.

☞ If you have been delayed, book an appointment with a doctor.

☞ Finding the confidence to say no when you are unable to do something instead of always agreeing right away.

3. **Monitor and record your workouts and physical movements**: Write down the physical activities you do, like playing sports, doing exercises, or going on long walks. Please keep track of how much time you spent doing the training and add whether or not you liked it. Here are some easy ways to get more exercise without even realizing it. For example:

☞ Park further from the store so that you will get a chance to walk a bit longer.

☞ Do not take the elevator; just climb the stairs. I know some of you immediately said absolutely not. Sometimes you are going to the first floor; you can take the stairs here. If you have a disability, then that is understandable.

☞ Take your pet for a walk.

☞ If you have children and they play sports, do not stay seated the entire game; stretch your legs and move around a bit.

☞ If you are a golfer, instead of using a golf cart, you should walk around the golf course.

☞ If you have a bicycle and the store is near, ride instead of walking.

4. **Remember to be grateful**: Write down the things you feel thankful for today. You might be happy today because you are not feeling any more soreness from your workout, you can see your family, or you have the option to work remotely. Focusing on being thankful can change how you see life. Other ways you can show gratitude every day are:

    ☞ Thanking someone. Make sure to say thank you to someone today. You have the option to do this either face-to-face or by sending an email or text message. Let them know you like and value what they do. Describe how their actions and work improve your life and the lives of others.

    ☞ Take time to be present and appreciate the good things in your day.

5. **Write how music makes you feel**: Make a note of any music you listened to today that helped you feel more positive. Normally, cheerful tunes can improve your mood. The happy melody and words can make your brain release chemicals that make you feel better. Think about making a list of happy songs that make you feel positive about life. Look back in your journal and listen to these songs when you feel sad or need some extra energy in your day.

6. **Write down anything that makes you happy or brings you joy in your positivity journal**: Who made you crack up today? Was it a person on YouTube? Or someone at work who did something hilarious. If anyone had a good experience, write

about it in your positivity journal. When you read it again, it will definitely make you laugh.

7. **Think about whether you can adapt to changes easily and if you can bounce back from difficult situations**: Did you and your partner have a disagreement when you found out they did not make a reservation in time for the restaurant you love as they promised? Were you open to finding another place to eat so that the date could still happen? Or did you demand to go home? Life always has unexpected things happen. Flexibility means being able to change your plans or actions when things unexpectedly occur. When unexpected problems happen, you don't get discouraged, but instead, you bounce back fast and complete the task.

8. **Why don't you write about the food you had today in your positivity journal?** Maybe you tried something new and discovered that you liked it. Or perhaps you had dinner at your mom's house, and she made your favorite pasta dish. If you enjoyed every delicious bite, it's worth writing about. Remember when we spoke about practicing mindfulness when eating? Try it out here.

9. **So, what was the thing you did not like the most today?** Perhaps you had to do tasks, and you really disliked doing them. Or maybe you had to go to the dentist or take your cat to get groomed. Everyone has things that they do not really like. Write about it to let go of the negative feelings.

10. **What made you feel happy?** What did you have fun doing today? Did you take your kids to the pool

and have a great time? Did you and your friends have brunch with a few mimosas? Did you and your partner go kayaking? Or maybe you went to the gym with a friend after not going for many months, and it was nice to catch up. No matter what you did, describe how it made you feel.

Toxic Positivity

As much as I am promoting positivity and encouraging you all to tap into it, I ensure that it addresses real issues and realistic and practical ways to approach this. However, there is a thing called toxic positivity. It is hard to believe, I know. But it is a very real thing. It tends to occur with some people who go looking for positivity from an unrealistic perspective and have gone into the fairytale aspect of positivity, which is not real. I want to spend time discussing what toxic positivity is, identifying it, if you may be doing it, and how to deal with it when it is coming from other people. When you see someone that you know going through a difficult period, like losing their job, going through serious financial constraints, being diagnosed with a serious illness, or experiencing the death of a loved one, you might be tempted to tell them to think more optimistically. Having a positive attitude is always beneficial, right? But it may not always be the case. Studies show that constantly feeling the need to be positive can have negative consequences and cause harm. This is known as toxic positivity. From reading this book, I am sure you may be aware that not all positivity is toxic. When you have hope and believe that things can get better even when things are difficult, that is called helpful positivity. This is where you apply all the tools listed throughout this book, and they have started to become part of you. On the other hand, toxic positivity wants you to ignore all your negative feelings, basically not truly dealing with them, instead placing them in a box and putting them on a shelf and acting like they do not exist, and this can be harmful for your well-being (I will explain more on that later on).

Examples of Toxic Positivity

Toxic positivity is something that happens a lot, so you have likely experienced it before—either in the way you see things in your own life or in how someone else responds to a situation you are going through. These are some phrases you may have heard before that sometimes come from toxic positivity:

- ☞ Take this time and look at the bright side

- ☞ Change your mood; you will bring yourself and everyone done

- ☞ Oh well, everything happens for a reason.

- ☞ Do not worry

- ☞ It will all work out. So why stress yourself?

- ☞ You stress too much; try stressing less

- ☞ Relax; you will get over this

- ☞ This too will pass

- ☞ It could be worse

- ☞ At least you are still here

When you first hear them, these may seem like nice or even useful things to tell someone who is unhappy. Now, if it is a day that you forgot your sweater to bring to work because it is usually cold at the office, hearing phrases like these might not seem important. It is completely normal and genuine to have a positive attitude towards a situation that is neither negative nor positive. The issue is when being positive does not match the situation and makes the other person feel like their feelings are invalid. To know if positivity is good or bad for you, watch out for signs that may indicate it is harmful. Pay attention to how you speak to yourself and how you interact with others. Feeling pressured to have a specific emotion is not good, even when it seems like the reminders are happy. Feeling ignored when you come across toxic positivity makes you feel bad and can make you feel like you are playing for team negativity when you truly are not. It can make your true emotions feel as if they are not acknowledged or made smaller. You end up feeling small or unimportant. Toxic positivity is like an oversimplified view of a complex situation. It ignores the challenges you are encountering. Inappropriateness means something that is not suitable or appropriate, while a feeling that being upbeat is off-base means feeling that being happy or cheerful is not the right thing to do in a certain situation. The background is very important, and not every situation needs to be seen in a positive way. Toxic positivity means being overly positive and optimistic in every situation, even when it is not helpful or realistic.

What Causes Toxic Positivity?

Exposure to societal expectations and our social circle are common sources of our understanding of toxic positivity. Helping someone feel better in the midst of their struggles is often pushed as the norm, leading us to believe in its merit. However, this can stem from the pure intent to offer assistance. Struggling to provide solace to those most affected by an unfortunate event is not uncommon. Dealing with the tough stuff and truly forming connections with others is a challenging feat, whereas toxic positivity may appear more effortless. However, the latter can lead to feelings of isolation and a lack of support, making difficult situations even more arduous to handle.

How Can Toxic Positivity Affect Your Health and Well-Being

Positive and optimistic attitudes generally have a positive impact on health, a principle I have consistently advocated for. However, it is important to recognize that toxic positivity can be detrimental to your well-being:

1. **Toxic positivity represents an extreme viewpoint**: Toxic positivity can hinder your ability to express genuine emotions, making it more challenging to cope with intense feelings. It is crucial to avoid toxic positivity because it involves dismissing and trivializing your true emotions, which ultimately proves unhelpful in the long term. In fact, attempting to suppress your emotions can intensify them further, leading to a loss of control. Constantly maintaining an overly positive demeanor can induce feelings of shame.

2. **Toxic positivity instills guilt and shame**: By invalidating your emotions, making you feel childish and overly reactive. Toxic positivity can force you to adopt a false persona, discouraging authenticity.

3. **Embracing an artificial positive outlook can undermine the significance and validity of your normal human experiences**: It is essential to acknowledge your emotions, learn how to address them, and never resort to pretense. Toxic positivity can also generate feelings of loneliness and isolation. When someone dismisses your concerns or worries, you may believe that you are the only one experiencing such negative emotions. Consequently, you may refrain from sharing your feelings with others, leading to increased feelings of solitude and a reluctance to seek support. Constantly maintaining an overly positive mindset can decrease your proactivity. Believing that a smile alone can resolve challenging situations may lead you to ignore problems and avoid taking the necessary action to overcome them. To combat toxic positivity, it is crucial to allow yourself to acknowledge and express difficult emotions, regardless of the circumstances, rather than suppressing or ignoring them. Listed below are some recommendations for handling situations where others or you display toxic positivity.

Dealing With Toxic Positivity From Those Around You

Ignoring toxic positivity or responding with a simple phrase like "Alright, thank you" is often the best approach. However, in close relationships where you seek better support from the other person, you can try these techniques. Acknowledge their intention to be helpful. Many individuals who display toxic positivity genuinely want to be supportive, but their approach may not be effective. Explain how their words impact you. It's important to remember that people who consistently strive to be overly positive may not realize that their words can be hurtful. It is generally acceptable to let them know that their comment did not seem helpful. Provide alternatives or suggest different actions they can take. Clearly communicate whether you want them to listen, give advice, or assist with a specific task, such as bringing lunch.

Addressing Toxic Positivity in Yourself

If you find yourself engaging in toxic positivity without being helpful, whether towards someone else or yourself, strive to adopt a more compassionate and empathetic approach. Before regurgitating automatic phrases and terms, take the time to actively listen. Pause what you're doing, remain silent, and give the person your undivided attention. This demonstrates your genuine concern for them and your desire to comprehend their experiences. It's crucial to listen without immediately responding with positive statements, as this may not address their true needs. Sometimes, simply being present and attentive can be more valuable than trying to offer comforting words. When you have a toxic positive mindset towards your own situation, it's important not to dismiss or ignore your negative emotions. Failing to acknowledge or attend to feelings of sadness, loss, fear, or anger doesn't lead to improved well-being. Instead, focus on becoming aware of your emotions. Seek clarification and ask questions before taking any actions. Understanding someone's feelings is vital before attempting to find a solution to their problem. If you feel inclined to downplay your own emotions about something, try acknowledging and accepting those feelings instead. When conversing with others, prioritize understanding and supporting their emotions and circumstances before rushing to solve their problems.

Here are some suggestions for phrases you can use:

- ☞ That sounds really difficult

- ☞ I do understand why you feel like this.

- ☞ I understand why you feel this way. I would also feel unhappy as well.

- ☞ I am here for you; I will not be leaving your side

- ☞ I am available if you need support

I hope that bringing this to light will allow you all to be a bit more mindful before speaking to others and yourself. The truth is, many times, we have been conditioned to say these terms and phrases, and they are not coming from a bad place. However, before saying things, we must first listen. Also, many of us practice this when speaking to ourselves, and I just want to remind you all that I want you to be realistic and practical. Positivity is not about ignoring everything and smiling all the time as if nothing is ever wrong; that is not how we are designed. It is about being in the present and finding different ways to approach certain things that occur in our lives. Always remember to be patient and kind to yourself.

Conclusion

I wrote this book from a place of understanding, and I wanted to help those of you out there who would benefit from tapping into the positivity code. The ideas and various techniques I presented to you are not merely theories; when put into practice and you remain consistent, they are effective. I was able to do it, and I believe that you can as well. When you tap into believing in yourself and being patient with yourself, you will be surprised at what you are able to achieve. You have the fortitude and discernment to create the life you want for yourself. There is so much in you that you have not yet discovered, and once you are ready to step into that zone, you will see for yourself. I want to leave you with two main things to reflect on as you embark on this new journey in your life, and that is to reflect on body positivity and embrace your new and lifelong journey with positivity.

Reflecting on Body Positivity

Many times, how we view our bodies affects us in a variety of ways, and they can sometimes be quite negative. It can be so negative that, in extreme cases, there are people who end up with body dysmorphia. This can lead to eating disorders. When it gets to this stage, the person can only see themselves in a particular way, even though that is not what they really are. They may look in the mirror and see themselves as severely overweight, but they are actually slim. This sometimes occurs with people who lose a lot of weight and are on their path to getting healthy. They are haunted by the image of what they once looked like. I want to take this time to delve into body positivity. It allows you to gain a deeper understanding of it and, for those of you who may view your bodies in a negative way, allows you to shift your mindset a bit. The body positivity movement has been something that has been promoted a lot on social media and television ads in recent times, and it has been giving people who have been thinking they look odd a chance to see that they are not and how to love and appreciate themselves more. When talking about body acceptance, there are two main viewpoints that people often discuss. Some people believe in body positivity, which means they love their bodies no matter how they look, how big or small they are, what color they are, what gender they are, or what abilities they have. Some people believe in body neutrality, which means they focus on being grateful for what their body can do. It may be beneficial to strive for a balanced combination of both.

Body positivity means that every human being should feel good about their body, no matter how society or popular culture thinks they should look. The body positivity movement has a few main goals:

- Changing the way society thinks and views the human body.

- Promoting the idea that all bodies should be accepted.

- Assisting people in feeling more confident and accepting of their own bodies.

☞ Dealing with unrealistic expectations for the perfect body.

Body positivity is about more than just challenging society's judgments of people's physical size and shape. It also acknowledges that there are people who are often judged based on their race, gender, sexuality, and disability. Body positivity is about helping people understand how messages in popular media affect how they feel about their bodies. It includes how they think about food, exercise, clothes, health, who they are, and taking care of themselves. By learning more about how these influences affect us, the goal is for people to have a better and more realistic relationship with their bodies. As many people set unrealistic goals that can be healthy and damaging and do not set realistic times to lose weight and get frustrated when they do not do it, body positivity does promote patience and love for yourself and your body.

Quick History Lesson on Body Positivity

Body positivity comes from the idea of accepting and celebrating all body sizes and shapes. It began with the fat acceptance movement in the late 1960s. Fat acceptance is about stopping the mean and unfair treatment of people with larger bodies or more weight. The National Association to Advance Fat Acceptance started in 1969 and still works to change the way people think and talk about weight. It encourages them to not focus on unhealthy ways, such as strict dieting or excessive exercise, to lose weight. The body positivity movement, which many of you may be familiar with, started around 2012 and was mainly about questioning unrealistic beauty expectations for women. As more and more people gravitated towards body positivity, they started talking about how all bodies are beautiful instead of just accepting different weights. Even though body positivity means accepting and loving your body just the way it is, regardless of societal beauty standards, others may see it as advocating for representation and inclusivity of all body types in media and society. Overall, body positivity aims to promote self-acceptance and celebrate the diversity of bodies. Depending on who you speak with about it, it can mean:

- Loving and accepting your body, even with imperfections.

- Feeling good about how your body looks

- Valuing and taking care of yourself.

- Being okay with the way your body looks, regardless of how big or small it is.

- Body positivity means being happy with your body and not feeling bad about any changes that occur naturally because of getting older, having a baby, or the way you live your life.

Instagram, which is a widely used social media app, was very important in helping the body positivity movement become more popular. In the past few years, many magazines and companies have tried to promote body positivity in their magazines and advertisements. Some magazines no longer change the appearance of models in photos, and companies like Dove and Aerie have made advertising campaigns that promote body positivity.

Reasons for Body Positivity

One important aim of body positivity is to talk about how the way we think about our bodies affects our mental health and our overall happiness. When people feel good about how they look and value themselves, it is because they tend to have a healthy body image. Studies show that if someone views their body negatively, it can lead to more mental health issues, like being very sad or having trouble with eating. What your body image means is how you personally see your own body, even if it is not how it really appears. How you feel, think, and act about your body image can greatly affect your mental health and how you treat yourself. You will tend to be more harsh and say very negative and mean things to yourself as a form of encouragement to get you to work on your body, but in the end, it does way more harm than good. The development of how we see and feel about our bodies begins at a young age. Unfortunately, even very young children can feel unhappy with how their bodies look. Difficulties that can arise due to negative thoughts about your appearance include:

- ☞ **Depression**: The depression rate is higher in women than it is in men. Some studies believe that feeling unhappy with your body may be a reason why women are more likely to be depressed than men.

- ☞ **Low self-esteem**: Studies have discovered that teenagers, regardless of their gender, age, weight, race, ethnicity, and how much money their family has, feel bad about their bodies, and this makes them have low self-confidence. Once there is no contentment with how they physically appear, everything is off for them.

☞ **Eating disorders**: studies show that when people are not happy with their bodies, they are more likely to develop eating disorders. This is especially true for teenage girls who deal with being bullied about their weight and constantly comparing themselves to celebrities and other people around them on social media. Many teenage girls already desire to have surgical procedures, even before the age of twenty-one. Teenage boys are affected by the need to either be slim or athletic, and they also compare themselves to people on social media and develop unhealthy, unrealistic body goals.

Studies have repeatedly shown that when people see images of what society considers a very thin body as ideal, they tend to develop behaviors and emotions related to eating disorders. Looking at these images is not the only problem. The real danger is when people start believing that being thin is what makes someone beautiful, successful, and respected. Studies have also shown that when people start believing these thoughts, they are more likely to feel unhappy with their bodies and go on diets that are not needed. Body positivity aims to help people understand the factors that lead to feeling negative about their bodies. The idea is that once people understand the root of this, they will change their ideas about how their bodies should look and feel more comfortable and okay with their own bodies. Accepting yourself can help improve your mental and physical health by fighting against the negative effects of having a poor body image.

Issues That People Find With Body Positivity

Whereas there are great intentions behind this movement, I have to be fair and also include the criticisms that this movement has faced. Although body positivity aims to make people feel good about themselves, it still has some issues and faces disapproval. For instance, one issue is the belief that body positivity means people should do whatever they feel is necessary to feel good about their appearance. Sadly, many people are constantly told that being thin and fit makes them happier, healthier, and more attractive. This belief in being thin can cause people to do unhealthy things like exercise too much or go on extreme diets while thinking they are being body-positive. Another problem with body positivity is that it might not include everyone. Images or representations promoting a positive body image often do not include individuals who are not white, have disabilities, identify as LGBTQ, or identify as non-binary. People usually see certain types of bodies as beautiful in body-positive messages. This makes some people feel left out and not included in the body positivity movement. Another problem with the body positivity trend is that it focuses too much on how a person looks, which can make them overly concerned about their appearance. This can create a whirlwind of confusion. Someone may feel that if the movement is about being positive about your body and accepting it, then why focus so much on how they look? This aspect ignores the other parts of a person's identity that are more significant than their appearance. We should not judge our worth based on our appearance. This could be a better way to include everyone.

So What Can You Do?

Body positivity is about learning to accept and love your body, which is great, and I am for that. However, sometimes it can be difficult and challenging, which are all human emotions and are normal to have. You are not being negative this way, but if you are not careful when adopting this new mindset of body positivity, you can dive too deep and make yourself feel like you have to meet very high expectations. The message of body positivity is that you should learn to be happy with your body, but it can also feel like another thing you have to do. Encouraging people to just accept themselves and stay strong against the constant pressure from images promoting a slim body can actually be harmful. Telling people not to pay attention to society's popular standard of beauty is actually not practical. It can make someone who already feels worried, sad, and unimportant feel even worse. The things that are commonly liked in society make people think they have faults but also expect them to act positively about it. If you do not feel good about your body, it can make you feel ashamed and guilty. Studies have shown that when people who do not feel good about themselves try to convince themselves of unnaturally positive things, it usually doesn't work and makes them feel even worse than before. Remember, I keep telling you about being realistic, and this is why. We are not about the superhero level of positivity; it is just not achievable. It is still *very* important to say nice things and have positive thoughts about yourself.

A better way would be to focus on replacing negative thoughts with thoughts that are more true and accurate:

1. Pretending to be positive when you are not is not necessarily a good idea. Faking it till you make it does not work with positivity. What can you do to feel good about your body? Whether or not you agree with the body positivity movement or not, there are some ideas that it presents that might make you feel better about yourself and care less about trying to be perfect.

2. Adopt a body-neutrality approach. It is okay to acknowledge that you do not really like everything about your body. It is alright to feel neutral or indifferent about your body. Your value does not depend on how you look or your body shape or size. Body image does affect how we perceive ourselves, without a doubt, but it is not the most important thing. Try not to think too much about your body and instead focus on other aspects of yourself when thinking about who you are. All of these things are challenging, but they are doable, and you can do it. I am not saying it just because I feel like it is a fact. Especially after taking the time to apply the techniques I left throughout this book. However, it is going to take a lot of effort, and consistency is going to have to be your best friend. There will be times when you do not feel strong enough and do not like things about yourself, especially when you find yourself comparing yourself to other people. This is why you should not do that. The important thing is to keep trying the different ways I listed on how to

stop thinking negatively, quiet that inner critic, and squash that worry bug that all contributes to making you feel bad about yourself and your body.

Try Health-Focused Self-Care

Self-care is often thought of as a way to alter or manage how you may be feeling about yourself. Let me make it clear that self-care is a good thing, and I have encouraged you to do this. In this context, there are many people who feel that only getting massages, etc., would eradicate all the negative feelings that they are having about their body. But, as you have now discovered, negative feelings are psychological, and they need various things and techniques to help shift your mindset into team positivity. Some of you have not addressed the underlying issues, which is why after partaking in retail therapy, spa days, pedicures, etc., you may end up feeling sad and having more issues with your body. Take care of your body and treat it. You must take care of your mind, which is also a part of you, as your body and mind are on the same team, but your dominance, because of how you feel or think about yourself, affects how you perceive yourself. It is important to eat nutritious food because it gives energy to both your mind and body. Exercise to feel strong and energized, not to change or control your body. Choose and purchase clothes that fit and flatter your body instead of buying for a future body shape or size that you hope to have. You might keep your "thin clothes" because you hope to lose weight in the future, but this can make it difficult to feel confident in yourself right now. Search for things that make you feel relaxed and happy with your appearance. Get rid of clothes in your closet that do not fit you well anymore. Your body might get bigger or smaller in the future, but that does not mean you should not feel good about yourself right now. Remove or unfollow accounts on social media that make you feel bad about yourself. If you often compare yourself with others, it is harder for you to feel good about yourself. You should follow accounts that you find interesting and that make you feel happy.

Teaching Children to Develop a Positive Body Image

If you have kids, here are some ways you can help them feel good about their bodies. Sometimes, we say various things about our bodies, and we do not even notice how our words can change how our young children view themselves:

1. Please, let us stop talking about diets around children. This is about feeling unhappy with how your body looks. Diets make you think you need to change how you look, and kids often understand this too. Now, nothing is wrong with taking on a new and healthy approach that will become a part of your life, but if you are talking about getting into a quick-fix diet and saying things like "I am so fat I need to lose my tummy," around your child who has a little tummy, they are going to think they need to lose their tummy and that they are super fat when they are not.

2. Always keep in mind that your children are hearing and paying attention to everything you say. They take in and mirror how you discuss your body. The more positive and neutral words of acceptance you speak, the higher it is.

3. Wear clothes that make you feel confident about your body. This means that you don't have to adorn or embellish your body. You can wear clothes that make it easier for you to move around and help you feel calm and comfortable. When your child sees you doing something, they will do the same thing.

4. Teach children to pay attention to how their body works instead of how it appears. You can do this by saying things like, "Wow, your hair is healthy," or "Your eyes are so good they do miss a word when you are reading" (instead of just saying that they are beautiful or handsome). Nothing is wrong with telling them that; however, if that is all you tell them, that is all they will focus on, you understand?

5. Make sure you know what your kids are looking at on social media. Think about whether the pictures and messages you are seeing are promoting feeling good about your body or not. Do not ignore it when they are being critical of their own body. Set a good example and show your children how to talk about your body using words that are positive or negative.

Embracing Positivity as a Lifelong Journey

Your positivity journey does not have a timeframe, meaning you will just need to do this for a year or six months. This is forever, forever, forever. This will have to be something that you decide has to be in your life until you take your last breath. This is a lifestyle change. So it is a part of you now. What you will notice as time progresses is that certain things that took you a while to react to in a positive way will not take that long again. This is a part of you for a lifetime because life will present new challenges. So, in this beautiful and crazy world filled with all different obstacles, it is important to stay positive in order to have a happy and satisfying life. Being positive is important because it helps us face new challenges with a different mindset, deal with difficult situations, and enjoy the little things in life. This way of thinking helps you grow as a person, become stronger, and have a more positive outlook on life. I will leave you with reminders that you must never forget.

The power of having a positive mindset—positive thinking is a powerful tool that influences how you feel, what you do, and how healthy you are in general. When you have a positive mindset, you can discover opportunities even in difficult situations. Instead of focusing on failures or obstacles, we use them as opportunities to learn and improve ourselves. If you think about the positive things in life, it can help you feel less stressed, have better relationships, and take care of your mind and body.

Making you feel better and think more positively. Negativity can make you feel drained and harm your mental and emotional health. But being positive helps protect you from negative feelings or thoughts. It helps you turn bad thoughts into good ones. By staying positive, you can feel calmer, handle pressure better, and become more mentally resilient. It helps you stay positive and think clearly when you have problems so you can find answers and make good decisions. Building better relationships means working on ways to create stronger connections with others. It involves putting effort into improving communication, understanding each other better, and building trust and respect. This can involve actively listening to others, showing empathy, being supportive, and being open and honest in our interactions. When we build better relationships, we can create deeper connections and have more fulfilling and satisfying interactions with the people around us. Being positive is crucial for creating and taking care of relationships. When you have a positive attitude, it attracts people who think the same way about your life. People who have positive attitudes are easier to talk to; they are more empathetic and nice, which makes people feel safe and supported around them. If you have a positive attitude, you can make good connections with others, solve problems without fighting, and make your relationships with your loved ones stronger. Being positive also helps you forgive and forget about being angry at someone and promotes getting along better with others.

How to be successful and grow as a person—having a positive attitude is strongly related to achieving success and developing as a person. When you have confidence in yourself and think positively, you are more likely to put in effort and keep going towards your goals. Positivity helps us stay motivated to overcome problems, adjust to new situations, and view challenges as chances to improve. If you have a positive mindset, you are more likely to be open to learning, trying new things, and doing things that make you uncomfortable. This not only makes it more likely for you to succeed but also makes your experiences better and helps us see things from different angles.

Steps to Not Forget When Embracing Positivity

Embracing positivity takes time and effort, but you can learn to do it. Just take it one day at a time. Here are a few things you should not forget on the positivity journey:

1. Be thankful for the good things in your life every morning when you wake up. This helps you think more about the good things in your life. (Gratitude)

2. Positive self-talk means replacing self-doubt and negative thoughts with positive affirmations. Stay positive and believe in yourself when things get tough. (Do not give the negativity tree any fuel.)

3. Surround yourself with happy and encouraging people who make you feel inspired. Reduce the number of negative influences and interactions in relationships and media. (You are in control; do not compare yourself to others; and find a positive group.)

4. Focus on the present moment and appreciate the beautiful things around you. Do things you like that make you happy and calm down. (Also, practice mindfulness meditation.)

5. Assisting others. Doing kind things for people creates good effects. You can help out by volunteering, listening to others, or offering help whenever you can. (This will help add to your sense of purpose.)

Embracing Positivity During Difficult Times

Practicing positivity is great and all, but I know some of you are still worried about how to keep this practice going during really difficult times. No need to worry (bye, bug). I will be including a few steps that you can apply to your life when faced with difficult times.

1. Try to think positively and find new ways to look at things. Pay attention to the positive things. Our brains tend to focus more on negative things. It tends to ask us, "What else?" when we are going through a lot, which can have a big impact. It does not mean ignoring difficult things, but it helps us focus on the good. Use positive self-talk. Find a phrase that you can say to yourself to feel better, such as "I am trying my best at this moment." Remember that in most situations, you have the power to choose your thoughts and how you will react. If you think negatively, it makes it harder for your brain to naturally fight off depression. Think about a recent negative experience you had. You could choose to think of it as a big deal or a small deal, depending on how you saw it. When we have a disagreement with someone who is angry, it can make one person's day worse than another person's day. This happens because of the way we talk to ourselves in our minds during and after the argument. Equip yourselves with the information provided to silence negativity the minute it enters the chatroom.

2. Pay attention to things that you have control over. Accept and be okay with what other people are or are not doing in the present moment. We can share information and make suggestions, but we cannot make other people do things our way. Helping and being kind to each other and ourselves will make it easier for all of us to do well during tough times. Keep in mind: When people feel stressed, they might not think clearly and may not be polite. It is important to remember that almost everyone is

going through tough times, and keeping this in mind can help you be nice and show understanding towards others.

3. Think of the bigger picture. I know this seems cliché, but this is actually applicable here. Try to see things from a bigger point of view. Things like not believing something or ignoring something have always existed. Understand and realize that even though this moment might be hard or hurtful, the next moment can be better. We have all experienced hard times that were eventually followed by better times. And by doing the same thing, making an effort to realize that your current experience is good (or at least not bad) can help you appreciate this more fun time instead of ignoring it.

4. Take care of yourself and treat yourself well. When we feel really upset, it is important to remember that our reactions do not mean we are "bad," "difficult," or "inferior." It just means we are human beings. Self-compassion is extremely important for us to develop resilience. Having people in your life who support you and are there for you is really important. Make sure to ask for and give help when needed. It is important to have a good balance between work and personal life to avoid getting too tired. Being drained and burned out will never work for anyone.

5. Embrace fun and relaxing activities. Sometimes, when we feel sad, depressed, angry, or stressed, we tend to stay away from the activities or actions that we know can make us feel better. For example, when

we feel stressed, we often become less active and isolate ourselves more. This reduces our energy levels and makes it difficult to think about anything other than our problems. This is a good time to practice mindful meditation because doing certain breathing exercises can be very beneficial. You can also combine deep breathing with positive thoughts, for example, "Breathe in: say I embrace today." Or say, "I let go, and I welcome the future." "Breathe out: say when I take a breath, I realize all the things I can do." When you breathe in, you become aware of my own truth. And you express your true self when you exhale.

6. Deciding to shift your mindset to that of positivity can improve your life, making you happier and more satisfied. By having a positive attitude, you can give yourself the strength to face difficult situations, make good connections with others, and become a better person. It is something that you are going to need to work on and put effort into, but the benefits are very much worth it. You will not regret making this decision.

Chapter "Good Will"

Your Chance to Inspire

You have the power to make a huge impact on someone else's life and help them step towards a future of true fulfillment. All it takes is a few words.

Simply by sharing your honest opinion of this book and a little about your own story, you'll show new readers where they can find all the guidance they need to set forth on the path toward their best life.

Helping others without expectation of anything in return has been proven to lead to increased happiness and satisfaction in life.

I would love to give you the chance to experience that same feeling during your reading or listening experience today...

All it takes is a few moments of your time to answer one simple question:

If so, then here is my small request from you again.

If you've found value in your reading or listening experience today, I humbly ask that you take a brief moment right now to leave an honest review of this book.

It won't cost you anything but 30 seconds of your time—just a few seconds to share your thoughts with others.

Your voice can go a long way in helping someone else find the same inspiration and knowledge that you have.

Are you familiar with leaving a review for an Audible, Kindle, or e-reader book? If so, it's simple:

If you're on **Audible**: just hit the three dots in the top right of your device, click rate & review, then leave a few sentences about the book along with your star rating.

If you're reading on **Kindle** or an e-reader, simply scroll to the last page of the book and swipe up—the review should prompt from there.

About the Author

Chrío Zoë is a passionate personal development guru. She has written several books on helping people escape their comfort zones and unleash greater versions of themselves. She believes that everyone should have the mind to ferociously pursue and achieve better versions of themselves. True freedom lies in permitting yourself to fly. She hopes that this book will inspire you to unclip your wings and start flying to the greater altitudes that you are meant to be at.

This author has a knack for capturing the essence of life's complexities, intricacies, and universal truths through her writing, often presenting thought-provoking perspectives on various aspects of existence.   Her life books are characterized by rich character development, as the author skillfully weaves together the stories of diverse topics, illuminating journeys, challenges, and triumphs. Through books, the author explores themes such as love, passion, victory, identity, personal growth, and the search for meaning, offering readers profound insights and moments of introspection.

Beyond Zoë's professional accomplishments, she also has a rich and multifaceted life outside of publishing. This book is a testament to her commitment to providing valuable insights and practical guidance. The author's books are often praised for their ability to evoke empathy in readers, fostering a deep connection between the readers and the valuable insights they encounter within the pages.

The author is a distinguished authority in various fields of study, bringing a wealth of knowledge and experience to her thought-provoking non-fiction works. As you delve into Zoë's manuscripts, you can expect to embark on an intellectual journey guided by Zoë's profound insights and intentional thought-provoking passion for self - development.   Her non-fiction works continue to push the boundaries of knowledge, inviting readers to expand their horizons and gain a deeper understanding of life and its impact on our success.

Zoë's works have been praised for their meticulous research, insightful analysis, and the way they challenge readers to think critically about the world around them.

Any one of Zoë's latest books....

1. Unlocking Infinity: Master the Art of Longevity
Learn How to, Boost Your Brain Health, Recharge Your Immune System and Restore Youthful Balance in 3 Easy Steps

2. Living Your Best Life: Radiate from Within
Ultimate Guide to Finding Purpose & Fulfillment in 3 Easy Steps.

3. Redefining Aging: The Art of Living Alone
How to Find Joy in Independence, Live Fearlessly & Maintain Longevity

4. Longevity: The Art of Aging Backwards

Step-by-Step Guide to Renew, Restore and Reverse Aging Mentally, Physically & Spiritually

5. Journeying Alone, Journeying Strong: Navigating Aging Alone Without Children

Self-Help Guide to Finding Inner Strength, Peace, Joy & Fulfillment in Childless Aging

6. Alone, But Not Lonely: Aging on Your Terms

A Roadmap for Aging Independently, Striking Balance & Finding Purpose

7. Mastering the Steps to Success: Achieving Success at Every Rung

Proven Strategies for Overcoming Obstacles and Reaching Greatness. Develop, Learn, Succeed

8. The Growth Mindset Code: Cracking the Secrets to Success

Comprehensive Guide to Breaking Limits with A Growth Mindset, Cultivating Unlimited Possibilities

9. The Superfood Prescription: Refuel Your Mind & Body

100 Supercharged Foods to Revitalize & Transform Your Health

... is another testament to her dedication to delivering enlightening and captivating non-fiction literature. Whether you're a seasoned reader of non-fiction or new to the genre Zoë's work is sure to engage, inform, and inspire.

To stay updated on **Zoë Publishing's** latest projects and musings, visit us on **facebook.com/zoepublishing** and follow us on Instagram & Tik Tok **(@zoepublishing)**

References

American Psychological Association. *Inferiority Complex.* APA Dictionary of Psychology. https://dictionary.apa.org/inferiority-complex

Benefits of mindfulness. (2023, February 23). Helpguide.org. https://www.helpguide.org/harvard/benefits-of-mindfulness.htm

Brown, J. (2023, September). *10 positive thinking myths that are actually keeping you stuck in life.* Ideapod. https://ideapod.com/10-positive-thinking-myths-that-are-actually-keeping-you-stuck-in-life/

Butler, K. (2022, April 6). *12 Benefits of writing in a positivity journal every day.* Power of Positivity. https://www.powerofpositivity.com/positivity-journal-benefits/

Cherry, K. (2020, November 21). *What is body positivity?* Very Well Mind. https://www.verywellmind.com/what-is-body-positivity-4773402

Christian, L. (2021, July 13). *How to believe in yourself (in 5 simple steps).* Soul Salt. https://soulsalt.com/how-to-believe-in-yourself/

Create your own happiness: cultivate a positive mindset. (2023). Practicing Positive. https://www.practicingpositive.com/create-your-own-happiness-mindset/

Edberg, H. (2023, March 22). How to stop being a people pleaser: 7 powerful habits. The Positivity Blog. https://www.positivityblog.com/stop-being-people-pleaser/

Erickson, E. (2023, May 12). *All about toxic positivity: definition, health effects, and how* health/toxic-positivity/guide/

Farnoosh. (2019). *Get to know yourself: 29 questions to discover the real you.* Prolific Living. https://www.prolificliving.com/get-to-know-yourself/

5 Habits to embrace positivity during hard times. (2022). Atrium Health. https://atriumhealth.org/dailydose/2022/01/25/5-habits-to-embrace-positivity-during-hard-times

Itani, O. (2020, March 2). 8 *Steps to help you stop overthinking everything.* Omaritani. https://www.omaritani.com/blog/stop-overthinking

Positive thinking: Stop negative self-talk to reduce stress. (2022, February 3). Mayo Clinic. https://www.mayoclinic.org/healthy-lifestyle/stress-management/in-depth/positive-thinking/art-20043950#:~:text=Lower%20levels%20of%20distress%20and,from%20cardiovascular%20disease%20and%20stroke

Positive thinking strategies to help you achieve your goals. (2023). Gaiam. https://www.gaiam.com/blogs/discover/positive-thinking-strategies-to-help-you-achieve-your-goals

Ritzhert, C. (2022, October 19). *What to know about an inferiority complex.* WebMd. https://www.webmd.com/mental-health/what-to-know-inferiority-complex

Sherwood, A. (2022, January 16). *What is positive thinking?* WebMd. https://www.webmd.com/mental-health/positive-thinking-overview

Spano, M. (2022, November 29). *The Power of Positive Thinking: Changing your thoughts can change your life.* The Hofstra Chronicle. https://www.thehofstrachronicle.com/archive-2012/the-power-of-positive-thinking-changing-your-thoughts-can-change-your-life

What's the difference between body positivity and body neutrality? (2022, April 22). Cleveland Clinic. https://health.clevelandclinic.org/body-positivity-vs-body-neutrality/

Why do I feel inferior? How to overcome an inferiority complex. (2021, August 13). My Online Therapy. https://myonlinetherapy.com/why-do-i-feel-inferior-how-to-overcome-an-inferiority-complex/

Wooll, M. (2021, October 15). *How to stop worrying: 11 steps to reduce stress and anxiety.* Better Up. https://www.betterup.com/blog/worry

Writes, P. (2023, June 29). *Embracing positivity: the key to a fulfilling life.* Medium. https://priyankavivek315.medium.com/embracing-positivity-the-key-to-a-fulfilling-life-68fd6c979262